GLACIER'S

A PICTORIAL HISTORY OF THE HOTELS AND CHALETS OF GLACIER NATIONAL PARK

GRANDEST

PRESENTATION OF THE PEN USED TO SIGN THE WATERTON-GLACIER INTERNATIONAL PEACE PARK AGREEMENT, 1932. LEFT TO RIGHT: H. ALBRIGHT, CANNON MIDDLETON, E.T. SCOYEN, AND THE HON. SCOTT LEAVITT. Glacier National Park Photo

The Call of the Mountains

Vacations in
Glacier National Park
Waterton Lakes National Park

GLACIER'S

A PICTORIAL HISTORY OF THE HOTELS AND CHALETS OF
GLACIER NATIONAL PARK

GRANDEST

BY BRIDGET E. MOYLAN

"See America First"
GREAT NORTHERN RAILWAY
Glacier National Park
1914

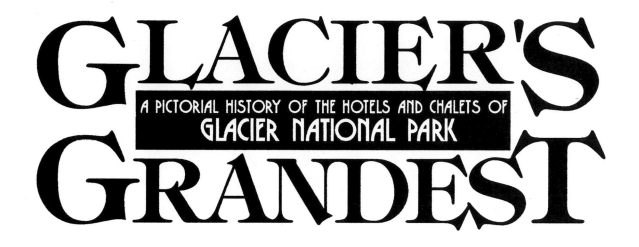

SEE AMERICA FIRST · GLACIER NATIONAL PARK
1922 to 1935

GREAT NORTHERN RAILWAY
GLACIER NATIONAL PARK
1921

GREAT NORTHERN
1936

GREAT NORTHERN RAILWAY
1936

1967

PICTORIAL HISTORIES PUBLISHING COMPANY, INC.
MISSOULA, MONTANA 59801

LIBRARY OF CONGRESS
CATALOG CARD NUMBER 94-67154

ISBN 0-929521-89-7

First Printing: May 1995
Second Printing: May 1996
Third Printing: April 1997
Fourth Printing: April 2000
Fifth Printing: April 2004

PRINTED IN THE U.S.A.

Typography: Leslie Maricelli
Layout: Stan Cohen
Cover Layout: Mike Egeler, Egeler Design

Cover art from a 1920s Great Northern Railway brochure.
Back cover postcards from the collection of Stan Cohen.

PICTORIAL HISTORIES PUBLISHING COMPANY, INC.
713 South Third Street West, Missoula, Montana 59801
E-mail - phpc@montana.com
Website - pictorialhistoriespublishing.com

Contents

CHAPTER ONE: THE HOTEL CONCESSIONERS

FROM RAILS TO ROADS 1

CHAPTER TWO: GLACIER PARK LODGE

A GRAND BEGINNING 15

CHAPTER THREE: LAKE MCDONALD LODGE

WEST GLACIER'S GLORY 27

CHAPTER FOUR: MANY GLACIER HOTEL

GLACIER'S GEM 37

CHAPTER FIVE: THE ERA OF THE CHALETS

HAVENS THAT WERE 51

CHAPTER SIX: GRANITE PARK AND SPERRY CHALETS

HALLMARKS OF HISTORY 65

CHAPTER SEVEN: PRINCE OF WALES HOTEL

THE ELEGANT CANADIAN 71

CHAPTER EIGHT: MOTOR INNS

TRAVELLERS' RESPITE 75

CHAPTER NINE: THE RED BUS FLEET

A WHEELED REVERIE 77

REPRISE 79

PRESENT DAY PHOTOS OF THE HOTELS 80

BIBLIOGRAPHY 87

"DEDICATED TO THE EMPLOYEES OF GLACIER NATIONAL PARK
—PAST AND PRESENT—
LET THE TRADITION CONTINUE!"
-B.E.M.-

PREFACE

Scattered among the rugged peaks, jagged rocks, the rumbling creeks and alpine lakes of Waterton-Glacier International Peace Park stand many architectural treasures. These buildings are remembrances of one man's vision, and they have reached the hearts of millions of visitors.

By 1891, the Great Northern Railway's Marias Pass route, skirting the southern border of what would become Glacier National Park, was a brand new addition to Montana. The territory had gained statehood only two years previously, and tourism was not yet a byword, but the seeds were being planted that would make tourism a future Montana industry.

Louis W. Hill became president of the Great Northern Railway in 1907. He saw his railway and the potential establishment of Glacier National Park as two interlocking puzzle pieces. Glacier became a national park in 1910, creating for Hill the perfect destination for Great Northern touring car passengers. Hill began to tailor the railroad's advertising campaigns, taking tourists westward. Slogans such as "See America First" and "The National Park Route" encouraged Americans to look inward instead of abroad for recreational possibilities. The railroad opened up the "frontier," and those with even a small spark of curiosity came to see the acclaimed sites. In many ways, the Great Northern Railway made Glacier National Park an overnight success.

Hill knew that the wealthy clientele he attracted would expect exceptional accommodations, with the Great Northern's ready access to the park. Because there was only one hotel inside the park, the Lewis Glacier Hotel (now Lake McDonald Lodge), Hill needed to build other accommodations, especially on the eastern side. Constructing Glacier Park Lodge and several backcountry chalets was Hill's initial focus, with Many Glacier Hotel and the Prince of Wales Hotel to follow.

Glacier Park Lodge was completed in 1913, establishing the Great Northern's first park stop from the east. By the end of 1914, the Great Northern had built the largest hotel in the park, Many Glacier Hotel, as well as nine chalets. With the exception of Belton, the chalets were accessible primarily by boat or trail. Hill's last structure, the Prince of Wales Hotel, was completed in Alberta, Canada in 1927, thus setting the stage that would bring the two parks closer as Waterton-Glacier International Peace Park on June 18, 1932.

The ownership of the hotels and chalets (excluding Lake McDonald Lodge) has changed twice since the Great Northern Railway constructed and began operating them in 1912.

In 1961, the hotels and chalets were sold to independent owner Don Hummel, and operated as Glacier Park Incorporated. Under a 25-year contract the concessions were sold again in 1981 to a subsidiary, Dial Corp. (formerly known as

Greyhound Corporation). Under these ownerships, various concessioners have contracted to operate the facilities, but the Great Northern is still remembered as founder of the concessions in Glacier. Today the Waterton-Glacier International Peace Park contains four concessioner hotels, two chalets, three campstores, and three motor inns.

Perhaps the best way to learn about this bygone era is to let history speak through the people who lived it. This book relives those times through pictures and remembrances of those who were guests and employees of Glacier's Grandest.

In this pictorial book we will travel through almost a century of the great hallmark structures, glimpsing those that were and those that still are in existence; their construction, the visitors who have walked their halls, and the employees who have dedicated their summers to the park. I hope you enjoy this collection of Glacier's past as much as I have enjoyed gathering it in this book for you.

– Bridget E. Moylan

The rendezvous for the Eaton Party was last summer at Glacier Park Station on the Great Northern Railway. Getting to that point, remote as it seemed, had been surprisingly easy—almost disappointingly easy. Was this, then, going to the borderland of civilization, to the last stronghold of the old west? Over the flat country...the train of heavy Pullman diners and club car moved steadily toward the west.

Then at last, at twilight, Glacier Park Station and Howard Eaton on the platform and an old Chief Three Bears, of the Blackfeet, wonderfully dressed and preserved at 93...It was rather a picturesque party.

I confess that no excursion...gave me a greater thrill than the one that accompanied that start the next morning from the Glacier Park Hotel to cross the Continental Divide.

Mary Roberts Rinehart
Through Glacier Park, 1916

CHAPTER ONE

THE HOTEL CONCESSIONERS
FROM RAILS TO ROADS

The designers for the railroads became quite adept at creating in their architecture the 'image' the railroads needed to provide distinction to the resorts. After all, the railroads wanted to create places worthy of 'writing home about'—places where the hotels were nearly as memorable as the scenery.

National Register of Historic Places

*T*he Great Northern Railway, with its vision of a railroad line to the Pacific Coast, saw the potential in attracting travelers with a railroad line skirting Glacier National Park. The railroad believed Montana offered a vacation destination that was unique and adventuresome. The Great Northern's extensive publicity was targeted at Americans who generally took lengthy trips to Europe. They tapped into this market and lured Americans to Glacier with their catchy slogan, "See America First." Glacier National Park, with its spectacular grandeur and fine lodging, was the appeal. The conveyance to the park would be the Great Northern Railway's touring cars.

The Great Northern Railway was instrumental in preserving the mountainous area in Montana's northwest corner as Glacier National Park. The *Saco Independent* from the Eastern Montana Highline reported, "Largely because of Louis Hill's enthusiasm for and love of this area, in which he had hunted and explored, the railway provided substantial leadership in promoting legislation which established Glacier as a national park in 1910."

While Glacier National Park was gaining a reputation as America's newest national park, Hill's Great Northern scurried with blueprints for impressive dining, lodging, and recreational facilities. The railroad spearheaded its project by designing, building, and operating a network of grand hotels and quaint backcountry chalets.

It was not in the railroad's earliest dream to manage hotels, but the directors of the Great Northern realized that the appeal had to be spectacular if it were to attract the railroad traffic they desired. Louis W. Hill stated at the 1911 Yellowstone Conference: "We do not wish to go into the hotel business; we wish to get out of it and confine ourselves strictly to the business of getting people there, just as soon as we can. But it is difficult to get capital interested in this kind of pioneer work." Hill recognized that the demand for fine facilities was certainly prevalent, and since the Great Northern was the only evident source of the needed capital, it naturally became the concessioner.

MUCH BUILDING IN GLACIER PARK

BIG TOURIST TRAVEL FORCES
BETTER ACCOMODATIONS. AND
BETTER TRAILS

Washington, October 16.—Tourist travel to Glacier national park was so extraordinary this year that the government is building a twenty-five mile automobile highway from St. Marys lake to Lake McDermott in order to make accessible to automobile stages what is regarded as the most picturesque spot in the Switzerland of America. Work already is being rushed on this new road which is to link the $100,000 meandering automobile highway built by Louis W. Hill, chairman of the Great Northern railway, from Glacier park station, the eastern gateway of the park, to St. Marys lake, a distance of thirty-two miles. This will make a continuous automobile highway extending fifty-seven miles into the mountain recesses of Glacier park. More than a score of automobile stages will be put in service during 1914.

More than eleven thousand tourists visited this newest of the nation's parks this year, setting another record for all the rest of Uncle Sam's playgrounds, nearly twice as many as were there last year. And yet the Rocky mountain park is only in the third year of its existence. Cheap transportation and low hotel rates, government officials declare, are making Glacier park the most popular people's resort in the country.

To keep pace with this unusual flow of tourist trvel, the Great Northern railway is erecting three new Swiss chalet hotels which will be opened next year. A 110 room annex to the huge hotel at the eastern gateway now is in course of construction and two 100-room picturesque log hotels are being built in the wilds on the shores of Red Eagle lake and Lake McDermott.

Besides this activity on the part of the railway, which already has spent more than a million dollars in the development of the "park on the roof of the continent," the United States government, as the result of Secretary Lane's visit there this year, is making wide "boulevard trails" over the great divide in three place. Gunsight. Swift Current and Piegan passes. This assures safe horseback travel over the top of the continent three different ways.

WORK STARTS ON BIG HOTEL IN THE GLACIER NATIONAL

Great Falls, April 15—In preparation for the entertainment of the large number of sightseers who are this season expected to visit Glacier National Park, the new playgrounds of the nation, work has already been commenced by the Great Northern towards the erection of its proposed hotel at Midvale, the entrance to the new park. After having made a visit at Midvale where he looked over the preliminary work in connection with the improvements to be made in that vicinity by the Great Northern, President Louis W. Hill left for St. Paul yesterday. General Superintendent C.O. Jenks, of the central district, met Mr. Hill at that place and was with him during the inspection, returning to this city yesterday.

The hotel to be constructed at Midvale will be about 200 by 100 feet in dimensions and will be a most artistically designed structure to be built mainly of logs somewhat similar in style to the forestry building at the Seattle exposition. Already 50 car loads of logs have been received at Midvale for use in this structure, some of the logs being of such proportions that no more than two could be placed upon a car. Some of these logs are no less than six feet in diameter and as a number of these are to be used for pillars in the main lobby, which pillars are to be 52 feet in height, some idea of their immensity may be gained.

In addition to the large lobby, dining room, kitchen and other public rooms, the hotel will contain about 100 guest rooms. The structure will be most artistically decorated in a manner in keeping with its rustic style and the whole will well accord with the rough grandeur of its scenic setting.

It will be modern in every respect and will be provided with a supply of crystal pure water to be brought through a pipe line extending back into the mountain a distance of about 7,000 feet. The pressure will be furnished by gravity and after passing through the hotel the excess flow will be run through a turbine wheel which will operate a dynamo to furnish electric lights for the building.

The hotel will cost not less than $75,000 and will be built by Evensta & Co., contractors of Minneapolis. The contract provides that the building shall be completed and ready for occupancy by the first of August.

In connection with the building of the hotel, Guthrie & Co., Great Northern contractors, have already started the construction of a magnificent automobile road which will extend through the reservation for a distance of 40 miles, from Midvale to the edge of the park, seven miles from St. Mary's Lake. From this point on to the lake the road will be built by the government.

Daily Inter Lake, April 15, 1912

"The White Men are Coming"

THE irresistible call of the glorious West is being answered from all over the world. Glacier National Park—America's newest and grandest scenic playground—*awaits you!*

Come! *Come this Season!* Your comfort has been amply provided for. A magnificent new hotel, one of the most novel and interesting institutions of its kind in the country, has just been completed. Every room is electrically lighted and heated. Every modern feature including shower baths and plunge pool, has been installed. The cuisine is worthy of the finest Eastern establishments. The rates—American plan $2.00 to $5.00 a day.

Tours Through Glacier Park

By Automobile, Horseback, Launch, Stage and Afoot—$1 to $5 Per Day

Whether you decide simply to stop over for a few days on your trip to or from the Pacific Coast or whether you plan to stay for several weeks, you will find that ideal arrangements have been made to enable you to transform every minute of your stay into a perfect memory. Ideal accommodations are offered by the famous chain of Swiss Chalet Camps throughout the Park.

Aeroplane Map Free Write for unique Aeroplane Map in colors and complete descriptive booklet and travel literature free, or apply to any Chicago, Burlington and Quincy or Great Northern representative.

124

H. A. NOBLE, Gen. Pass. Agent,
Great Northern Railway
Dept. 103   St. Paul, Minn.
Panama-Pacific International Exposition,
San Francisco, 1915

Heeding his own advice, Louis W. Hill wasted no time in beginning construction of the hotels. In June of 1912, the builders began raising timbers for the Glacier Park Lodge at Midvale (now East Glacier). The lodge at East Glacier, the chalets, and the Many Glacier Hotel were all built between 1911 and 1917, with the Prince of Wales Hotel at Waterton in Canada completing the two parks' accommodations by July 1927.

Most of the Great Northern's holdings were on the east side of the park with the exception of the Belton Chalets at Belton (now West Glacier). Lake McDonald Lodge, then known as the Lewis Glacier Hotel, was built in 1913 by private owners and did not become part of the concessioner operations until the National Park Service purchased it in 1930 and leased it to the Great Northern.

Louis W. Hill

Beginning in 1914, the concessions were managed and operated by the Glacier Park Hotel Company, a subsidiary of the Great Northern Railway. In 1943, the concessioner shortened its title to Glacier Park Company and continued to run the facilities until the railroad announced its desire to sell those holdings in 1951. The Great Northern agreed to continue operating the concessions until an owner could be found. The National Park Service expressed regret at the railroad's decision to part with the title, since the railroad had played such a major role in the park's founding. However, the Great Northern Railway could no longer rationalize its capital losses. Glacier National Park's hotels and chalets had not realized a profit since 1940 and were losing up to $530,000 a year. Previously, the railroad had offset its hotel and chalet losses with profit from the railway touring cars, but eventually, changes in transportation reduced that source of income as well. American tourists were no longer dependent on the railroad for transportation. Instead, automobiles and buses were carrying visitors to Glacier, significantly undermining the railroad's original interest in the hotels.

The Glacier Park Company noted: "Conditions have changed materially since we entered the park operations in 1913. At that time and for years thereafter the railway was the only means of reaching the park and it was felt that construction and operation of the hotels by us was necessary. The necessity for our operating the property has ceased to be of urgent importance. Travel habits have changed due to the automobile. For example, in 1950 Glacier National Park was visited by 485,000 persons of whom 9,000 arrived by train while in 1925 only 40,000 visited the park, but of these 12,500 arrived by train."

GREAT NORTHERN RAILWAY BROCHURE, CIRCA 1915.

ONCE THE GREAT NORTHERN RAIL-
ROAD HAD BUILT THEIR HOTELS, THEY
PROMOTED THEM AND THE PARK
THROUGH THEIR RAILROAD TIME
TABLES. BOB LOGAN COLLECTION,
MISSOULA, MONTANA

SEE AMERICA FIRST--GLACIER NATIONAL PARK

ENTRANCES TO PARK.

The park may be entered at two points; Glacier Park Station, Mont. the eastern entrance, or at Belton, Mont. the western entrance. Both points on main line of Great Northern Railway. Tourists can enter at one gateway and leave at the other, making continuous trip through park or enter at Glacier Park Station, make various tours and leave park at same point.

PARK ACCOMMODATIONS, HOTELS AND CAMPS.

The Glacier Park Hotel Company operates several hotels and log chalet camps in the park as follows:

Glacier Park Hotel, at Glacier Park Station (eastern entrance)—200 rooms, accommodations for over 400 people—electric lighted, steam heat, running water, rooms with private bath, etc., cuisine and service of highest order; has a plunge pool, shower baths, sun parlor, open camp fire lounging room and is located about 1000 feet from the depot, facing the mountains. Rates $3.00 per day, American plan; with bath $4.00 and $5.00 per day.

At Belton (western entrance) are located the Belton Chalets—a group of attractive buildings adjoining the railway with accommodations for 100 people. These chalets are for the convenience of people entering the park via Lake McDonald. Rates $3.00 per day, American plan.

In the interior of the park log chalet camps are located as follows, taking them in the order they are reached from Glacier Park Station:

Two Medicine Camp on Two Medicine Lake, Cutbank Camp in Cutbank Canyon, St. Mary Camp on lower end of St. Mary Lake, Going-to-the-Sun Camp at upper end of St. Mary Lake, Gunsight Camp on Gunsight Lake, Sperry Glacier Camp in Sperry Glacier Basin, Many-Glacier Camp on Lake McDermott, Granite Park Camp near Swift Current Pass (temporary tent camp). From Many-Glacier Camp there is a trail over Swift Current Pass—in some respects the most interesting pass in the Park—this trail leads directly to Granite Park Camp, a distance of nine miles. Distance between camps ranges from eight to 16 miles. Rates at all camps, $3.00 per day.

The camps consist of a group of log buildings, attractively located at the best scenic points. The architecture is of the Swiss chalet type—each building is heated with large stone fireplaces. The service is less conventional than at the hotel. The aim is to provide good clean beds, plain food, well cooked, plenty of it, and served in family style.

TEPEE CAMPS.

The Glacier Park Hotel Company will this season maintain tepee camps at Glacier Park Station, eastern gateway to the Park, and at Many-Glacier Camp on Lake McDermott, in the heart of the scenic region. At the Glacier Park Tepee Camp guests may enjoy all the privileges of the main hotel, procure meals in the dining room if desired, enjoy the swimming pool, baths, etc., at same rate charged hotel guests, or may, if they desire, secure supplies from Glacier Park Hotel Company store. Beds in these tepees will rent for fifty cents per night.

McDermott Camp will consist of a number of tepees located convenient to a central structure, which will contain a small store room, a dining room, kitchen equipped with utensils, and a cooking range. A camp attendant will have charge of the store and will sell food to the tourists. Each tepee will contain four comfortable beds and will be heated by a Sibley heater.

The object of this new departure is to give tourists an inexpensive means of sustenance. If the plan meets with the approval of tourists it will probably be extended to the other camps throughout the Park. Using these camps tourists will be enabled to tour the Park at a cost of one dollar per day or less.

HOTEL AND CAMP RATES.

Glacier Park Hotel, Glacier Park Station, $3.00 per day. Rooms with bath, $4.00 and $5.00 per day.

All Glacier Park Hotel Company's Chalet Camps, $3.00 per day.

Tepee Camps (beds) 50c per night.

Glacier (Lewis) Hotel, on Lake McDonald, Geduhn's Resort and Park Cabin Resort, on Lake McDonald, $3.00 per day.

All hotels and camps on American plan.

AUTOMOBILE TOUR RATES.

The Glacier Park Transportation Company maintains daily automobile service between Glacier Park Station and St. Mary Camp, on the following schedule:

2.30 pm	8.30 am	Lv	Glacier Park Hotel	Ar	11.30 am	6.00 pm
5.00 pm	11.00 am	Ar	St. Mary Lake Camp	Lv	9.00 am	3.30 pm

Rates: One way $3.00, round trip $6.00.

Round trip need not be made same day. One piece of hand baggage weighing not to exceed twenty pounds will be carried free.

Time for one way trip two hours and twenty minutes.

FOUR-HORSE STAGE SERVICE.

A daily four-horse stage service is maintained between Glacier Park Hotel and Two Medicine Camp. Distance twelve miles. Stage leaves in morning and returns in afternoon. Time for one-way trip three hours—fares one way $1.25, round trip $2.50.

Daily four-horse stage service, during season, betwee St. Mary Lake Camp and Many-Glacier Camp, on Lake McDermott, in both directions. One-way fare $2.50, round trip $5.00—distance by stage road twenty-five miles, time seven hours.

Frequent stage service is maintained daily between Belton Station and foot of Lake McDonald, connecting with launches for all points on the lake—distance three miles, time forty minutes fare 50 cents each way, $1.00 round trip.

RATES FOR GUIDES AND HORSES.

Saddle and pack horses and guides can be secured at Glacier Park Station, St. Mary Camp, Going-to-the-Sun Camp, Many-Glacier Camp, and at Lewis Hotel, on Lake McDonald, at the following rates:

Saddle horses .... $2.00 per day
Pack horses .... 1.50 per day

When parties travel with horses the park rules require that a competent guide be in charge. Rates for guides are:

Guide, including board and horse .... $5.00 per day

One guide can ordinarily handle five to six people; above that number an additional guide is required for at least every additional six people. The expense of the guides can be divided among the different members of the party, viz.: for a party of five people, cost of guide would be $5.00 per day, making the per capita cost $1.00 per day for each member of the party—or a total cost of $5.00 per day for board and lodging, saddle horse, guide and guide's expenses for each tourist.

Pack horses are generally used for the purpose of carrying the dunnage bags and extra clothing of the guests. They are not absolutely essential on the shorter trip of three to five days, but are a great convenience. One pack horse will usually suffice for a party up to ten or twelve people.

Horseback tours are the popular method of touring the interior of the park where roads are not constructed.

COST OF HORSE-BACK TOURS.

The following table shows cost per day for such tours for parties of two or more people, including all expenses at hotels and camps and guide and horse hire:

	Cost per Person per Day		Cost per Person per Day
1 person	$11.50	7 persons in party	$6.65*
2 persons in party	8.25	8 " " "	6.45
3 " " "	7.15	9 " " "	6.25
4 " " "	6.60	10 " " "	6.15
5 " " "	6.30	11 " " "	6.05
6 " " "	6.10	12 " " "	5.90

*Second guide is added.

The preceding table is based on the services of one guide for the first six people, two guides for seven to twelve people, and one pack horse. This includes guest's board, guest's horse, pack horse, guide's horse and board—practically all expenses. Additional guides or horses, would, if required, be furnished at regular rates.

COMPLETE CAMPING TOURS.

Glacier National Park contains many beautiful camping spots; camping tours, independent of hotels or Great Northern Camps, are preferred by some people. Brewster Bros., General Outfitters in Glacier Park, are prepared to furnish complete outfits at the following price for trips of ten or more days:

	Cost per Day per Person		Cost per Day per Person
1 person	$19.50	5 persons	$8.20
2 persons	11.75	6 "	7.50
3 "	9.15	7 "	7.15
4 "	9.10	8 " or more	6.80

Above rates include the necessary guides, cooks, horses, provisions, tents, cooking utensils, stoves and everything except blankets. Tourists are advised to bring their own blankets or bedding—or can purchase blankets from Brewster Bros. for $4.00 per pair, with privilege of returning same in good condition and securing rebate of $3.00 per pair.

WALKING TOURS, $1.00 TO $3.00 PER DAY.

Walking tours are enjoyable for some people who like the more strenuous form of a vacation trip. Great Northern Camps are located within a day's walk of each other, ranging from eight to sixteen miles apart. Walking tours can be made at a cost of $3.00 per day by using the Chalet Camps—or, if a small party take their own tent outfit and dispense with guides, and by using one pack horse to carry equipment, the trip can be made for $1.00 per person per day, provisions being purchased as needed from our camps and hotels.

LAUNCH SERVICE.

A large new launch, accommodating 120 people, is operated on St. Mary Lake between St. Mary Camp and Going-to-the-Sun Camp, on upper end—distance ten miles, time one hour—one-way fare 75 cents, round trip $1.50.

Frequent launch service is maintained on Lake McDonald between foot of the lake and resorts at the head of the lake—distance ten miles, time one hour—fare one way 75 cents, round trip $1.25. Connection at foot of lake with stage to and from Belton.

GUNSIGHT LAKE CAMP.

To the next camp, located on Gunsight Lake, is about nine miles and the trail for the most part is through a beautiful forest following the course of the St. Mary River. Gunsight Lake (5,775) is about one mile long and lies in a pocket formed by the joining of the bases of Fusilade Mountain (8,747), Gunsight Mountain (9,250) and Mount Jackson (10,023). From Gunsight Lake it is about three hours by horse or afoot to Blackfeet Glacier, the finest glacier in the Park and said to be the finest example of a glacier in the United States. It has an area of about five square miles, spread out over the north slope of Mount Jackson and Blackfoot Mountain (9,597). On the south slope of Mount Jackson is Harrison Glacier and on the south side of Blackfoot Mountain is Pumpelly Glacier. These glaciers, while separated now by the summit of the Continental Divide, were at some time in ages past all one solid ice sheet. The glaciers are at an elevation ranging from 7,000 to 8,000 feet.

SPERRY GLACIER CAMP.

The distance from Gunsight Lake Camp to Sperry Glacier Camp is about five miles in a straight line, but to get from one to the other we must cross the Continental Divide via Gunsight Pass. From Gunsight Lake Camp the trail starts upward along the north wall of Mount Jackson. The trail leads up along the side of Mount Jackson and is very picturesque. About two hours' traveling brings one to the summit of Gunsight Pass (7,900) and you are rewarded by one of the finest views imaginable. Gunsight Pass is simply a saddle or depression where Gunsight Mountain and Mount Jackson join each other. At the foot of the western slope is Lake Louise (5,914), almost a duplicate of Gunsight Lake. The trail drops down suddenly to the water's edge and another climb is made over the Lincoln Divide (7,000) and down again into Sperry Glacier Basin.

The glacier is reached by an hour's climb from the camp. It is not difficult of access and women and children make the journey easily. Its average elevation is about 8,000 feet. By crossing the glacier and moraine in front of it you can look down into Avalanche Basin, 4,000 feet below. It is an awe-inspiring sight—one can hardly realize the awful distance to the bottom of that tremendous chasm. A large portion of Sperry Glacier was at some remote period precipitated over the brink of the head wall. The present Sperry Glacier occupies a space formed by the junction of Edward Mountain, Gunsight Mountain, Fusilade Mountain and Mount Brown. The buildings at Sperry Camp are constructed of stone—timber not being available at this elevation.

LAKE McDONALD.

A six-mile walk or ride brings one to Lewis Hotel or Geduhn's Resort, on the north end of Lake McDonald. It is a steep trail, but a good one, the total drop in that distance being about 3,500 feet. Lewis Hotel is a comfortable hotel of rustic design. This is a convenient place to use as a starting point for trips to Avalanche Basin, Granite Park, and for tourists entering the Park at Belton, en route to Sperry Glacier, and the east side of the Park via Gunsight Pass.

Lake McDonald is the largest lake in the Park, being about eleven miles long and averaging about one and one-half miles wide. The view up the lake is unusually fine, being framed in by a series of attractive peaks, including Stanton Mountain (7,744), Mount Vaught (8,840), Mount Cannon (7,000), Mount Brown (8,541), and Edwards Mountain (9,055). An interesting trip is up McDonald Creek to Avalanche Basin, about nine miles. McDonald Falls and Paradise Canyon are seen on the way. The trail is an easy one all the way to Avalanche Lake (3,865), and frequent views of snow-capped peaks are to be had through the dense tree tops. Avalanche Basin is one of the best examples of a glacial cirque in the Park—the head walls rise up abruptly to a height of 7,000 feet. The prominent peak on the right is the Little Matterhorn (9,055), a part of Mount Edwards. At the top of the head wall is Sperry Glacier, which discharges its melting waters down the steep sides and into the lake. The lowest point at which one of these streams breaks over the precipice is about 2,000 feet above the lake. The streams vary greatly from day to day in volume, according to how fast the glacier is melting. Trout are plentiful in the lake.

GRANITE PARK CAMP.

Heretofore tourist parties crossing Swift Current Pass have had to camp out at Granite Park. This will not be necessary now, as a temporary tent camp will be located there this season.

By the establishing of this camp it is but two days' trip via Swift Current Pass from Many Glacier Camp to Lake McDonald.

Granite Park is an ideal camping place, as plenty of water and wood is available. Parties crossing the main divide via Swift Current Pass use this as a night camp. It is located under the protecting shelter of the Garden Wall at an elevation of 6,000 feet. From this location one gets an excellent view of Heaven's Peak (8,994), Clements Mountain (8,764), and Mount Cannon on the south, and looking north one can see the snow cap of Mount Cleveland (10,438), the highest mountain in the Park.

Swift Current is the most picturesque pass in the Park.

We will gladly make up special itineraries covering as many days as you desire. Write any Great Northern Agent.

Great Northern Adventure Land Vacations

There is no finer place in which to spend your summer vacation than the international playground—Glacier National Park and Waterton Lakes Park in the American and Canadian Rockies. Here the scenery and recreational opportunities are so varied that one may spend from a few days to a month or more and enjoy every hour. Excellent hotel and chalet accommodations are available.

We can arrange a summer trip for you which will provide for a stopover of any desired length in Glacier Park, as well as visits to the famed cities and resort areas of the Pacific Northwest: Spokane, Seattle, Tacoma, Portland, Vancouver, Astoria and Victoria—Mount Baker National Forest, Rainier National Park, the Pacific seaside resorts, Alaska.

Escorted all-expense tours are offered for those who prefer to travel in groups with an experienced tour conductor who attends to all details of travel at no added expense. Itineraries are offered which include Glacier National Park in combination with Yellowstone; Glacier and Waterton Lakes Parks in combination with Banff and Lake Louise in the Canadian Rockies; the Pacific Northwest and Alaska alone, or in combination with other resorts.

Vacation pleasures begin when you board the Great Northern Empire Builder or the Oriental Limited.

....

A. J. DICKINSON, P. T. M. 1931
Great Northern Ry., St. Paul, Minn.
Dear Sir:—
    I would like information which will assist me in planning my summer vacation trip.
    There will be.........................persons in my party, leaving about ....and returning home about...
    I would like to spend...........days in Glacier National Park.
    If I make the trip I would like to visit at the following places:

....

....

I have checked the following statements to indicate my vacation interests:
- ☐ I am interested in horseback riding.
- ☐ I would like information about Dude Ranching in the Rockies.
- ☐ I would like information about a trip to Alaska.
- ☐ I would like information about Escorted All-Expense Tours.

                    Yours truly,

....

....

....

In 1914, Louis W. Hill stepped down as president of the Great Northern, taking with him the railroad's attachment to and enthusiasm for Glacier National Park's hotels and chalets. As a member of the board, Hill kept his hand in Glacier's hotel building projects until he had built the Prince of Wales Hotel in Waterton, but his love for Glacier's hotels was not shared by everyone. Ray Djuff states in *The Prince of Wales Hotel*, "William Kenney, a subsequent president of Great Northern Railway, stated in 1935: 'We must rid ourselves of all these parasites as quickly as possible.'" The Great Northern's connection with Glacier had become loosely tied.

In 1957, concessioner duties were transferred to the Knutson Hotel Corporation of Minneapolis. In March of 1960, the Great Northern announced that its properties in Glacier National Park were up for bid. A spokesman for the Glacier Park Company assured the public that someone would operate the Glacier National Park hotels "no matter what. They are too important to the park to just close up," he reassured.

The Great Northern sought an owner who not only had the capital for the operation, but who also was interested in the national parks and desired to run park concessions. The railroad found such a buyer in Don Hummel. Hummel was then the 54-year-old mayor of Tucson, Arizona, and he also operated concessions at Mt. McKinley in Alaska, and at Mt. Lassen National Park in California. In 1961, Don Hummel established Glacier Park Inc., and he and his young family began running the facilities.

VISITORS TOUR THE EAST SIDE OF THE PARK NEAR ST. MARY LAKE, CIRCA 1920. Glacier National Park Photo

"Our first summer at Glacier was wonderful," Hummel's wife Genee recalls. "We stayed in a quiet cottage on Lake McDonald in West Glacier. The scenery is fabulous—breathtaking. The beautiful hotels each have a distinctive charm. The summer went all too fast."

Hummel described those beginning years as hard work, but rewarding and progressive—until 1964, when Glacier National Park experienced its worst flood on record. As he recalls: "The season was a tragedy because we had the flood of '64. I had 600 employees on the payroll, eating like only college kids can eat, and couldn't reach a single hotel except by helicopter. It looked pretty bad. Fifteen miles of Highway 2 gone; 13.5 miles of the Great Northern Railway bed gone. The bridge over the Middle Fork [of the Flathead River] was condemned; there was no way you could get into the park. We lost the water and sewer system at Many Glacier, the water system at East Glacier; we lost the sewer system at McDonald [Lodge] and about one third of the dining room and half of the kitchen. It was sort of a bleak time. I didn't sleep very much that year!"

But despite the setback, Hummel's vision for the hotels guided him forward. Under his direction, the hotels catered to the tourists with entertainment. There was a new emphasis on hiring employees with singing, acting, dance and musical abilities. With talented youth, the hotels began to stage full musical productions, to the delight of the guests. Many Glacier Hotel, under the management of Ian Tippet, earned its nickname, "The Showplace of the Rockies." Musicals such as *Oklahoma!, Guys and Dolls, The Music Man* and many others were performed on the downstairs stage. Employees dedicated their time off to rehearsals and production without additional compensation. They performed for the spirit, the fun, and the camaraderie. The entertainment also gave the guests a unique experience: they were vacationing in the midst of Glacier's rugged wilderness, and at the same time, being treated to polished productions with stage lights, costumes, and talented performers!

After 20 years as Glacier National Park concessioner, Hummel announced his desire to sell the properties: "It's been a constant battle attempting to not only pay off the facilities, but to try to upgrade them as well," he stated. In 1981, Dial Corp. purchased the concessions from Hummel.

In 1992 Dial, now Viad Corp. began various facelift projects. Before the 1993 season, the hotels were upgraded with new lobby carpet, and spruced up in time for Glacier Park Lodge's grandest highlight since Louis W. Hill's father, James J. Hill's birthday party brought 600 guests to the hotel. In June of 1993 the American Academy of Achievement's 32nd Annual "Salute to Excellence" weekend was held in East Glacier at Glacier Park Lodge, attracting over 700 movie stars, playwrights, scholars and business and political figures.

Offsetting the encouraging improvements in the hotels, 1993 also marked a sad turn for Granite Park and Sperry Chalets. In 1992, the Belton Chalets, Inc., concession permit expired and was not renewed by the National Park Service. In the summer of 1993, the chalets were closed for the first time since the Luding family gained the concession in 1954. The Environmental Assessment for the chalets published in November 1993, states, "The primary concern is that regulatory changes since the chalets' construction in 1913-14 now make utility system operations complex and expensive. Both chalets have substandard sewage and water systems, inadequate life-safety facilities, and the combination of high overhead and operating costs and minimal revenue-producing capability to sustain the traditional visitor service provided." After extensive restoration efforts, the chalets now meet current health and safety codes. In 1996, Granite Park Chalet was reopened as a hiker's shelter for the time being, while in 1999, Sperry Chalet opened with traditional services.

With the exception of the years spanning World Wars I and II when the concessions were closed, the hotels have operated continuously since they were built in the early 1900s. In all, they have operated for about 80 seasons, the buildings withstanding close to 90 high mountain winters.

Louis W. Hill's dedication to the park and his efforts in creating the hotels and chalets of Waterton-Glacier International Peace Park are still appreciated today. The structures he built in the park are visible hallmarks of the pioneering railroad era of America.

"1934 WAS THE YEAR PRESIDENT FRANKLIN D. ROOSEVELT WENT THROUGH THE PARK. IT WAS ON A SUNDAY, AUGUST 5, 1934. MY FOLKS CAME UP FROM KALISPELL AND WE WATCHED THE PROCESSION GO PAST THE CAMP. THE PRESIDENT AND HIS WIFE BOTH WAVED AT US!" DOROTHY RAY PRICE. Glacier National Park Photo

A RED BUS ROUNDS THE BEND AT "THE LOOP." HEAVENS PEAK IS IN THE BACKGROUND.
Glacier National Park Photo

WORD SPREAD OF AMERICA'S NEW VACATION
RESORT. IN 1912, 6,237 PEOPLE VISITED THE
PARK. BY 1913, PARK ENTRANCE RECORDS
BOASTED 12,130 VISITORS.

WHITE TOURING BUSES IN FRONT OF GLACIER PARK LODGE,
1930s. Glacier National Park Photo

*"The structure will be most
artistically decorated in a manner in keeping with its rustic
style and in accordance with
the grandeur of its scenic setting."*

The Daily Inter Lake
April 15, 1912

CHAPTER TWO

GLACIER PARK LODGE
A GRAND BEGINNING

I'd like to talk about the lodge itself. It was so beautiful. I remember the flower baskets hanging and swinging in the breeze. It was just so glamorous with the rolling lawns and people coming in and out...it was a rich man's park then. It was a real fancy thing.

Trudi Carleton Peek
Glacier Park Transport Company employee, 1947

*T*he Great Northern's "National Park Route" touring car rolls into the East Glacier depot, flue smoke billowing, air brakes hissing, its whistle sounding its grand entrance. Bellboys run for luggage as tourists step down metal rungs, setting foot on Montana ground. Some eager visitors hurry off to the luggage claim; others gather their personal bags. As they move off the platform, the newcomers gaze north at the spectacular East Glacier range which foretells Glacier National Park's mountainous splendor.

Directly ahead of the depot, down a long, flower-lined path, stands majestic Glacier Park Lodge. Touring cars are parked under an archway held high by immense timbers. More bellboys lead the newly arrived guests into the lobby, where the visitors gasp in awe.

Before them extends a vast lobby 200 feet in length and 100 feet in width. Outlining the center of the lobby stand 30 pillars, each a massive Douglas fir column with its bark still intact. The huge logs are of such girth that two people standing on opposite sides of a pillar would be hard-pressed to touch each other's outstretched arms. The log pillars rise 52 feet from the basement to the ceiling where skylights send down sun shafts in slants of afternoon light. At the south end of the lobby, there is a stone fireplace large enough to stand in; giving, when lighted, a truly inviting radiance on drizzly summer days. The lobby's alpine touch speaks of Glacier's rugged wilderness, but in a comfortable, protected setting. Glacier Park Lodge was a structure built on a grandiose scale that celebrated both individual and national dreams and reflected the grandeur of the park.

Glacier Park Lodge was the first of the hotels in the park constructed by Great Northern President Louis Hill. He began construction in April of 1912 with 75 workers, and completed the main structure 15 months later on June 15, 1913. The main building consists of the lobby, dining room, and 61 guest rooms, the doors of which outline the lobby in three tiers. Despite the hotel's grand scale, Glacier Park Lodge proved inadequate for the great number of visitors ushered to the park by the Great Northern Railway. Hill ordered construction to begin immediately for

IT IS SAID THAT THE GLACIER PARK LODGE WAS DESIGNED AFTER THE FORESTRY BUILDING AT THE SEATTLE EXPOSITION OF 1909. THE BLACKFEET INDIANS NAMED HILL'S FIRST HOTEL "BIG TREE" LODGE. Glacier National Park Photo

AN EARLY TOUR BUS IN FRONT OF GLACIER PARK LODGE. Montana Historical Society

an additional 111 rooms, almost doubling the lodge's original capacity. This annex was completed the following winter. The total construction cost of the hotel and annex was $500,000.

Because the timbers required for such a structure were larger than those found in Montana's forests, the Great Northern brought the trees to the construction site from Oregon and Washington. In all, 60 timbers ranging from 500 to 800 years in age were shipped from the Pacific Northwest. Each weighing approximately 15 tons and measuring 36 to 42 inches in diameter, these massive timbers were shipped one or two to a flatcar to Glacier Park Station. All of the timbers were used, Douglas firs in the lobby, and cedars on the outside veranda.

Helene Dawson Edkins, of the original family homestead at Midvale (now East Glacier), remembers the hotel's beginning days: "We were here all through the building of the lodge. They brought all the huge trees in, I believe from Oregon, each tree on a flatcar. I can remember, as a little kid about 12 years old going up to the hotel ...we'd go to the lodge in the afternoons...Hill made it more Oriental, which is out of keeping here, but he had Japanese lanterns and all that stuff. We used to go up there because they had cookies and tea every afternoon, until mother discovered it and then put a stop to that!"

Louis Hill was a man of business. He devised a perfect way to advertise the Great Northern's Glacier National Park connection. He planned the lodge's grand opening to coincide with a celebration commemorating his father, James J. Hill's 75th birthday. On June 15, 1913, Louis invited his father's friends and all the employees who had worked for the Great Northern in the previous 25 years to the "birthday party." Over 600 attended the elaborate banquet.

With such a grand opening, the Hills set the pace for Glacier Park Lodge. Of all the hotels in the park, Glacier Park Lodge has always been the host lodge. Its

HORSEMEN IN FRONT OF GLACIER PARK LODGE. Glacier
National Park Photo

LEADING UP TO THE MAIN ENTRANCE OF GLACIER PARK LODGE. From an original post card

I'd like to talk about the lodge itself. It was so beautiful. I remember the flower baskets hanging and swinging in the breeze. It was just so glamorous with the rolling lawns and people coming in and out. But you know, whenever the train came, we always tried to meet it. We'd walk down to the train station. Of course there were always Indians in full dress—Blackfeet Indians...and they were in their glory in their headdresses and the train would chug into sight. And of course I'm of the generation where trains were a big deal. It was a steam engine. You would hear the whistle announcing that it was coming. So we'd meet the train because it was something to do socially. Just to see the new people, of course. Kids and nannys—it was a rich man's park then. It was a real fancy thing. And of course the roadsters from Glacier Park Transport Company would meet the VIPs and the buses would be there because there weren't a lot of people that drove into the park at that time. And of course this is 1947 so we were still in a kind of depressed era after the war, but I remember the drivers meeting the people, helping them into the cars, and taking them to the hotel. That was always the big thing. And these were wonderful young men who were so polite, and they had been coached, of course, to be personable. They had been chosen to be special in every sense. There really weren't any motels at that time. It was all Hotels. I remember the people would go up there and be as impressed by the beauty of the area as I was—the flowers and lawns and so forth—and they were let out in front of the hotel, and they'd go in and register.

Trudi Carleton Peek
Glacier Park Transport Company employee, 1947

activities are more centered in and around the grounds. For example, it is the only hotel with a swimming pool or a golf course at present. This lodge has continuously received the largest groups of guests—from 820 boy scouts in 1935, to large physicians' conferences, to the 1993 convention of the American Academy of Achievement attracting over 700 dignitaries and celebrities.

Glacier Park Lodge is a hallmark of the Great Northern's beginnings in Glacier National Park. It has been the hub of all the concessions, setting the standard of high style and luxury. Perhaps it was the public's favorable reception of the lodge that gave Louis W. Hill the encouragement and determination he needed to see beyond the struggles and setbacks of building such luxurious accommodations in a remote and wild park. He continued to follow his vision, building Many Glacier Hotel, Prince of Wales Hotel and a network of nine chalets in Glacier National Park.

THE SOUTH END OF GLACIER PARK LODGE SHOWING THE MASSIVE TIMBERS USED IN THE LODGE'S CONSTRUCTION. Glacier National Park Photo

LOCAL RIDES IN THE VICINITY OF
GLACIER PARK HOTEL

The open country around Glacier Park Hotel affords
many attractive saddle-horse rides of from one to three
hours.

Rates per one-half day, one to four hours—
without guide - - - - - - - - - - $2.50

Rates per day, four to eight hours—without
guide - - - - - - - - - - - - - 3.50

FEES FOR GAMES AT GLACIER
PARK HOTEL

Eighteen holes of golf (including use of Putting
Green and Shower Bath) - - - - - - - $1.00
Use of Putting Green per hour, per person - - .50
Use of Tennis Court per hour, per person - - .50
Use of Bowling Green per hour, per person - - .50

1920s

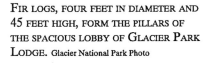

FIR LOGS, FOUR FEET IN DIAMETER AND
45 FEET HIGH, FORM THE PILLARS OF
THE SPACIOUS LOBBY OF GLACIER PARK
LODGE. Glacier National Park Photo

GLACIER PARK LODGE'S SPACIOUS LOBBY. Glacier National Park Photo

"Friends came out and we had horse shoes and dances, but usually we'd take them into the big hotel."

Charlie Jennings

REGISTRATION DESK AT GLACIER PARK LODGE. Glacier National Park Photo

CARRIED OVER FROM HIS "ORIENTAL LIMITED," LOUIS HILL INTRODUCED TOURING CARS...ADDING
AN ORIENTAL FLAVOR TO THE HOTELS WITH LOBBY LANTERNS AND TEA SERVERS. Glacier National Park Photo

MANY OF THE EMPLOYEES WERE HIRED NOT ONLY FOR THEIR PARTICULAR JOB BUT FOR THEIR MUSICAL ABILITY. Glacier National Park Photo

THIS IS POSSIBLY THE FIRST WOMAN TO LAND A PLANE AT GLACIER PARK LODGE. THE DETAILS, HOWEVER, ARE SKETCHY. Glacier National Park Photo

"BUT UNDER THE GREAT NORTHERN THEY HAD ENTERTAINMENT AT NIGHTS, YOU KNOW. THEY HAD A LADY (THAT)...USED TO BE THE HOSTESS THAT GREETED EVERYBODY. THEN THEY SHOWED PICTURES OF THE PARK." H.D. EDKINS. Glacier National Park Photo

THE LODGE STAFF IN THEIR EUROPEAN AND ORIENTAL UNIFORMS. Glacier National Park Photo

"SUMMERS WERE LIKE A BIG FAMILY REUNION IN THE EARLY DAYS OF THE PARK, AS MANY PARK VISITORS, EVEN THOSE WITHOUT CABINS, WOULD COME BACK YEAR AFTER YEAR AND STAY A MONTH OR MORE." BEA MACOMBER. Lake McDonald from an original post card

LAKE MCDONALD LODGE SITS ON THE EAST SHORE OF THE LAKE. From an original post card

Lake McDonald, Montana, reached only by the Great Northern Railway.

CHAPTER THREE

LAKE MCDONALD LODGE
WEST GLACIER'S GLORY

The trail led past the corral, past a vegetable garden such as our Eastern eyes had seldom seen. Under trees, around a corner at a gallop. Then the Glacier Hotel at Lake McDonald, generally known as "Lewis'."

There was good food. Again there were people dressed in civilized raiment, people who looked at us and our shabby riding clothes with a disdain not unmixed with awe. There was fox-trotting and one-stepping in riding boots, with an orchestra.

Mary Roberts Rinehart
Through Glacier Park, 1916

*T*oday, restaurants, gift shops, and gas stations are clustered about the West Glacier entrance playing host to the tourists who stream through the park daily in cars, camper trailers, and tour buses. Midsummer entrance numbers can reach thousands of visitors a day.

In the late 1800s, the west entrance to Glacier was no such "metropolis." In contrast, the entrance was shrouded and tree-lined with towering, many-centuries-old cedars. No bridge spanned the Middle Fork of the Flathead River until 1897, and not until 1911 did a rugged and rambling dirt road connect the river to the foot of Lake McDonald. Originally, all guests were rowed across the river and carried the two miles to the lake by buckboard. From there it was a 10-mile cruise to the head of Lake McDonald on Snyder's steamboat shuttle. It probably took a good part of a day to reach the lodge, if all equipment ran smoothly. Today, with the aid of bridges, asphalt, and the automobile one can drive from the West Glacier entrance to Lake McDonald Lodge in a leisurely 30 minutes!

The first families to reach the Lake McDonald area staked their homesites as early as 1892. Charlie Howe, Milo Apgar and Frank Geduhn were some of the original settlers at the foot of the lake. Later, many of them moved to the head of the lake, joined by Denny Comeau, George Snyder and Frank Kelly, all original settlers of the region. Because there was no farming in the area and the fur trade was not always profitable, these early residents started to cater to visitors who were beginning to explore the area, escorting them to Lake McDonald and on up the lake by boat. And so tourism started in Glacier's early days. The West Glacier hotel concessions can credit their humble beginnings to entrepreneur George Snyder who, in 1895, built the Snyder Hotel on the present site of Lake McDonald Lodge, 15 years before the establishment of Glacier National Park.

George Snyder, the first builder of a Lake McDonald-site hotel, was thought

GEORGE SNYDER'S FRAME HOTEL WAS BUILT IN 1895 ON THE SITE OF THE PRESENT LAKE MCDONALD LODGE. Glacier National Park Photo

"THIS JOHNY LEWIS WHO HAD A HOTEL HERE BEFORE THE PARK WAS OPEN, HE USED TO ENTERTAIN A LOT—IRVING S. COBB, CHARLIE RUSSELL AND WILL ROGERS. I GUESS THEY USED TO HAVE SOME PARTIES. WE NEVER REFERRED TO IT AS MCDONALD LODGE, JOHNY LEWIS' PLACE! AND ALL THE OLD-TIMERS REFERRED TO IT AS JOHNY LEWIS' PLACE. COURSE THERE ARE NO OLD-TIMERS LEFT. NOT MANY IN AND AROUND THE PARK." CHARLIE JENNINGS, HOMESTEADER AND SUMMER PACKER. Glacier National Park Photo

"IN THE SUMMER OF 1909, I VISITED LAKE MCDONALD, AVALANCHE BASIN AND SPERRY GLACIER IN THE COMPANY OF FOUR FRIENDS. WE WERE THE FIRST VISITORS FROM EAST OF THE MISSISSIPPI RIVER TO REGISTER AT JOHN LEWIS' HOTEL ON LAKE MCDONALD." J.W. DOWLER JOURNAL, 1935. Glacier National Park Photo

THE LOBBY IS THE MOST ARCHITECTURALLY SIGNIFICANT SPACE IN THE STRUCTURE. THE CONCRETE FLOORS ARE SCORED IN IMITATION OF FLAGSTONE AND HAVE INCISED MESSAGES IN BLACKFEET, CHIPPEWA AND CREE THAT TRANSLATE INTO PHRASES SUCH AS 'WELCOME,' 'NEW LIFE TO THOSE WHO DRINK HERE,' 'LOOKING TOWARD THE MOUNTAIN' AND 'BIG FEAST.' NATIONAL REGISTER NOMINATION FORM. Glacier National Park Photo

of as a "smart, worthless, old rich man" according to former West Glacier resident and famed local artist, Ace Powell. Because Snyder was tall and heavy, with a long thin neck and small head, "he was known as 'Gooseneck' by the locals," said early Lake McDonald resident Bea Macomber. Snyder ran the hotel for nine years before transferring ownership to John and Olive Lewis.

Genevieve Gudger, who spent part of her childhood at Lake McDonald, remembers the Snyder and Lewis Hotels. She recalls that Lewis won the Snyder homestead and hotel in a poker game. Other sources credit Lewis' wife Olive with gaining title to the hotel and the surrounding 285 acres between 1904 and 1906. However he acquired the property, John Lewis certainly had the foresight to recognize the need for accommodations on the west side of the park. He hired the architectural firm of Kirtland, Cutter, and Malmgram out of Spokane, Washington to design a new hotel that, in his words, was "something worthy of the park." Lewis moved the two-story Snyder Hotel back behind the building site, turning it into a general store.

Without any railroad or road service to the building site, it is truly a credit to Lewis for following through with what appeared to be a builder's nightmare. It was no easy task, but Lewis arranged to have the building supplies for the hotel hauled from Belton to the foot of Lake McDonald and then either ferried by boat in the summer or skidded 10 miles across the ice during the winter. Luck was with Lewis since Lake McDonald froze solid enough for traffic the winter of 1913, although on the average, the lake freezes over only once every four or five years.

Because the lodge was originally accessible mainly by boat, the front of the lodge faces the lake. The Architectural Preservation Guide for Lake McDonald Lodge states the rationale for the hotel's unique facing on the building site: "Quite naturally the building's most important elevation was at the west and faced the lake, since visitors arrived at the area by boat until 1920 when the road was constructed. The building was sited on a small rise above the water near the north end of Lake McDonald. Creating a suitable architectural entrance for the east elevation was never done, giving visitors, even today, the gnawing feeling that they are entering the rear of the structure, rather than the front." Therefore, today's visitor who drives in from the Going-to-the-Sun Road actually enters Lake McDonald Lodge by the back door!

Lewis purposely stayed in keeping with the Great Northern's Swiss design of a stone ground floor, wood frame construction, and alpine detailing on the outside shutters and balconies. Although a comparatively small structure with only 65 rooms, the lodge is equivalent in luxury to the other Great Northern hotels, and blends well with their motifs. Additions were never made to the main structure and the building retains to this day, its original cozy, hunting lodge atmosphere. In June of 1914 the "Lewis Glacier Hotel" opened for business.

Although John Lewis owned and operated both the Gaylord Hotel in Columbia Falls and the Lewis Glacier Hotel on Lake McDonald, his main business was the

THE BACK SIDE OF LAKE McDONALD LODGE (TOP) FACES THE ENTRANCE ROAD AND THE FRONT SIDE
FACES THE LAKE (BOTTOM). BOTH VIEWS ARE FROM THE 1930s. Glacier National Park Photos

fur trade. The lodge still reflects this early influence as many of Lewis' original "trophies" still hang from lobby timbers. Lewis was said to have bought furs from Joe Cosley, Charlie Howe and many others. It was well known that many of these furs were "poached" in the park, and one of the favorite trapping areas was up the McDonald Valley around Flattop Mountain. Former Belton resident Bud Henderson remembered a storeroom off the lobby of the Lewis Glacier Hotel that was stacked to the ceiling with furs of marten, mink, beaver, fisher and the rare otter. In the fall, when the hotel business was slow, Lewis would travel to New York to sell his furs.

As the fur business came to a halt, Lewis turned his attention to his lodge and to tourism. Heavier visitor traffic to the park increased the need for a more efficient access to the lodge. By April 1919, three and one-half miles of right-of-way were cleared and two miles of road were graded around Lake McDonald. By 1922 the entire nine miles of road were completed, making the lodge accessible by car.

From the west entrance of the park, where many passengers lodged overnight at the Great Northern's Belton Chalets, the trip to the Lewis Glacier Hotel catered to the select and adventurous few. In the spring of 1922 or 1923, Joe Opalka and his wife were part of the first car caravan that went up the new road along Lake McDonald to the Lewis Hotel. Driving their Saxon touring car, they were the second of a dozen cars. Joe states, "Cars often got stuck and every time this occurred the caravan would stop while men hopped out to help push the fellow out of the mudhole."

The drive from Belton to Fish Creek was through a dense cedar forest, on narrow, bumpy terrain. This scenic drive was swept out in the 1926 West Glacier fire and possibly in a 1929 fire. But today, the road is again tree-lined with 70-year "new" growth.

Unlike the other hotels inside the park, what became the Lake McDonald Lodge began under private, local ownership and remained locally owned for 35 years. However, in 1930 Lewis sold his hotel and the surrounding property on Lake McDonald to the National Park Service, which in turn leased the property to the Great Northern Railway. This title transfer brought all the hotels and chalets of Glacier National Park under one concessioner. It was at this time that the "Lewis Glacier Hotel" became Lake McDonald Lodge.

"AND THERE'S NO MORE ROMANTIC PLACE IN THE WORLD THAN LAKE MCDONALD IN THE MOONLIGHT. I CAN REMEMBER WHEN WE'D HAVE THREE OR FOUR ROWBOATS AT A TIME. AND SOMEBODY WOULD HAVE A UKULELE OR A GUITAR OR MAYBE AN ACCORDION, AND WE'D GET IN THE BOATS AND ROW OUT AND WATCH THE MOON COME UP OVER MT. BROWN, AND THEN WE'D ROW IN A WAYS AND WATCH IT COME UP AGAIN, AND WE WOULD WATCH IT COME UP FOUR OR FIVE TIMES DURING THE EVENING UNTIL IT REALLY GOT UP SO HIGH WE COULDN'T GET IN ANY MORE." BEA MACOMBER. Glacier National Park Photo

CHARLES M. RUSSELL
LAKE MCDONALD'S STORY TELLER

On the west side of Glacier there were permanent residents prior to the establishment of the park. Apgar was a thriving community of stores and cabins, and the families around the lake socialized often in the summer months, visiting each other's cabins or congregating in the evenings around the fire at the Lewis Glacier Hotel (now Lake McDonald Lodge).

The best-known character in early residence on Lake McDonald was Montana's famous artist, Charles Marion Russell. Russell is often referred to as the greatest painter of the American West. He and his wife Nancy built their Bullhead Lodge in 1896 near Apgar. Russell created numerous paintings and sculptures at his studio there, but storytelling was also his talent. A good friend of the Lewises, he would visit the hotel and attract a gathering of eager ears around the stone fireplace. (The 1949 *Glacier Park Drivers Manual* states that Russell etched the pictographs on the base and hearth of the hotel's original fireplace. Sadly, the fireplace was destroyed in the flood of 1964.)

Charlie was a familiar character to the residents of Lake McDonald. It has been said, "If he never painted a picture, he would have been famous for his stories." Russell and Irvin S. Cobb, who was an author and humorist, would often sit in the lobby of the Lewis Hotel and spin yarns. As the evening wore on, according to former Lake McDonald resident Genevieve Gudger, mothers would send their young daughters off to bed because the stories "could get pretty thick."

Cora Hutchings who had lived in the area since 1911, reminisces about the Russells and the Lewis Hotel: "We often spent an evening with Charlie Russell, the cowboy artist, and his wife Nancy...little dreaming that his collection of paintings would later be worth millions of dollars. He was a quiet, unassuming person. He always wore a colorful sash around his waist, a cowboy hat and boots. We would watch him sitting on the beach in front of his studio painting or modeling clay. However, I think we enjoyed him most at the close of the season when we would all sit around a large fireplace at the Lewis Hotel and listen to his stories. He had a seemingly inexhaustible number and a way of telling them so that even though we heard them over and over we still enjoyed them."

Charlie's friends from Glacier Park were among the last to see him alive. It was at Bullhead Lodge that he became ill. Cora Hutchings remembers: "It was the fall of 1926 that Mr. Russell was carried out from his home. He had been ill for a few days and we said goodbye to him while we waited for the train to take him home to Great Falls. We didn't think for a moment that we were not to see him again, but he passed away not long afterwards."

CHARLIE RUSSELL, THOUGH FAMOUS FOR HIS WESTERN REALISM PAINTINGS AND SCULPTURES, ALSO PORTRAYED A SENSE OF HUMOR IN HIS WORK. THIS CLAY AND STICK MAN IS HOLDING A JUG WHICH READS: "A JUG FULL OF GOOD WISHES TO MR. AND MRS. LEWIS FROM C.M. RUSSELL—1914." Glacier National Park Photo

CHAPTER FOUR

MANY GLACIER HOTEL
GLACIER'S GEM

We then packed up and hit the trail for Many Glacier. This is located in the heart of the park. It includes an immense rustic hotel and numerous small log chalets. The hotel is several blocks long, winding along the shore of a beautiful lake, with towering peaks on three sides. On the lake side of the hotel are spacious verandas from which one views the wonderful array of jagged snow-covered mountains. The hotel found favor in all our eyes and was much frequented by us, although the camp was two miles to the east....

Gordon Mettler
Park Visitor, December 1919

*I*n an unusually windless summer sunrise, Swiftcurrent Lake reflects the surrounding peaks. The Many Glacier Hotel stands amidst mountain shadows, and directly across the lake, Grinnell Point basks in alpenglow. Guests rest on the balcony or amble quietly along the shore.

The Many Glacier Hotel marks the end of a 12-mile road, the final destination of motor traffic. From Swiftcurrent Motor Inn and Campground there are only trails through the isolated valley. The Many Glacier Valley, tucked in a hidden pocket of the park, has always been Glacier's treasure trove.

The Many Glacier Valley, Louis W. Hill believed, was an idyllic setting for a grand hotel—a hotel that would hold its ground in the Crown of the Continent, under the wings of Mount Wilbur and Mount Gould, enclosed by the Ptarmigan and Garden Walls, and embracing the shores of Swiftcurrent Lake. Many Glacier Hotel was soon deemed the Showplace of the Rockies and it stands yet today as the largest hotel in the park.

Louis W. Hill conceived the idea of the Many Glacier Hotel before Glacier became a national park. In 1909 he selected the hotel site on the east shore of Lake McDermott (now Swiftcurrent Lake), knowing he would build his showplace there. Although the scenery was spectacular, at the base of panoramic peaks, the lake-front setting was inaccessible. In order to reach this pristine location, the crew had to build first a 30-mile road from East Glacier to Babb, and then 12 miles of road from Babb into the heart of the valley. By 1911, Hill had finished preparations for such a feat and asked the Department of Interior for permission to begin. His plan was approved with eventual reimbursement promised by the federal government and work began. Construction of the 53-mile connecting road progressed while Hill devoted his energy to building Glacier Park Lodge and the Belton Chalet.

© HILEMAN

"GO TO GLACIER NOW AND TRAMP OR RIDE HER WILDERNESS TRAILS AMID SURROUNDINGS REPEATED NOWHERE ELSE ON EARTH. CAMP BY THE WAY, OR STOP AT CHALETS...ABOVE ALL, TAKE TIME. AT SWIFTCURRENT LAKE ONE CAN PASS DAYS AND WEEKS WITHOUT LEAVING THE ENVIRONS OF MANY GLACIER HOTEL IN CONTEMPLATION OF MOUNTAINS, LAKES AND GLACIERS, WHICH YIELD GLACIER'S INMOST SECRETS..." *NATIONAL PARKS MAGAZINE* 1946, Montana Historical Society

"IF YOU WERE TO CITE ONE PLACE WHICH EMBRACES EVERYTHING IN THE FIELD OF THE SUMMER JOB FOR STUDENTS, IT WOULD CERTAINLY HAVE TO BE GLACIER NATIONAL PARK. MOUNTAINS, GLACIERS, LAKES, STREAMS, SUPERB FOREST SCENERY, A THOUSAND MILES OF TRAILS FOR FOOT AND PACKHORSE, PLUS LODGES AND HOTELS IN ABUNDANCE. THESE LODGES ARE STAFFED EACH SUMMER BY 800 COLLEGE STUDENTS WHO ARE THE BELLMEN, MAIDS, WAITRESSES, KITCHEN AND OFFICE WORKERS, INSTRUMENTALISTS, VOCALISTS, SINGERS, ACTORS AND DANCERS THAT KEEP HOTELS LIKE MANY GLACIER OPERATING."

Glacier National Park Photo

1920s

Table of Rates for All-Expense Tours
When Rooms with Bath are Used at Glacier Park
and Many Glacier Hotels.

Room with Bath at	Tour No. 2	Tour No. 3	Tour No. 4-A	Tour No. 4-B
$ 9.00	38.75	47.75	67.25	52.75
10.00	40.75	50.75	70.25	55.75
11.00	42.75	53.75	73.25	58.75
12.00	44.75	56.75	76.25	61.75

Room with Bath at	Tour No. 4-C	Tour No. 4-D	Tour No. 5	Tour No. 6
$ 9.00	58.00	51.00	76.25	85.25
10.00	62.00	54.00	79.25	90.25
11.00	66.00	57.00	82.25	95.25
12.00	70.00	60.00	85.25	100.25

EARLY VIEWS OF MANY GLACIER HOTEL, PROBABLY IN THE 1920s. NOTICE THE GLACIER PARK TRANSPORTATION COMPANY BUSES IN THE TOP PHOTO. Glacier National Park Photos

MANY GLACIER HOTEL ENTRANCE PRIOR TO THE PORTICO ADDITION. Glacier National Park Photo

NINE TOURING BUSES STOP AT MANY GLACIER AS BELLMEN GREET THE NEWCOMERS. Glacier National Park Photo

"I LOVED IT—IT'S JUST BEEN A PART OF ME FOR SO LONG... THE PARK JUST MEANS SO MUCH TO ME. I GO WHENEVER I GET THE CHANCE." GLADYS MILLHOUSE, MANY GLACIER EMPLOYEE, 1920s. Glacier National Park Photo

Soon after the completion of the road from East Glacier, the Many Glacier Chalet structures were the first buildings Hill constructed at the new site. The chalets were designed to accommodate saddle trips through the valley. In 1913, eight chalets were erected on the rising slope of Mount Altyn, above the future site of the Many Glacier Hotel.

Soon after the Many Glacier Chalets were up, groundwork for the hotel was underway. By the spring of 1914, construction had begun. As with Glacier Park Lodge, the large lobby pillars for the Many Glacier Hotel came from Oregon and Washington. Builders skidded the timbers by horse over the rugged new road from Babb. The medium-sized timbers were logged from the Many Glacier Valley itself. The logs were taken from the Grinnell Lake area upstream from the hotel and floated down Lake Josephine and Swiftcurrent Lake to the hotel site.

To prepare the lumber on site, Hill built a sawmill, a planing mill and a temporary kiln. From the Grinnell timber came the hotel's frame, siding, and original furniture.

Stone for the building's foundation was quarried on location as well. The exterior trim on the balconies and shutters was hand carved in the Great Northern's Swiss alpine detailing theme.

With 400 men working continuously, it took five months in early 1915 to complete the main, four-story structure. The Many Glacier Hotel was completed in June and opened on July 4, 1915, with a quiet celebration.

In 1917 the Many Glacier Hotel annex was added so that the hotel buildings followed the shoreline a total of 900 feet to the south.

The Many Glacier Hotel was a haven of luxury. By 1918 the hotel housed a swimming pool, tailor shop, barber shop, hospital, lobby telephones, hot and cold running water and steam heat. Authentic Japanese lanterns lighted the timbered lobby and a small orchestra played after dinner. In April 1957 a lakeside terrace and dance pavilion were proposed to be built adjacent to the St. Moritz Room, but the plan never made it past the drawing board.

On August 10, 1925, National Park Service Director Stephen Mather visited Many Glacier and saw that the sawmill used to build the hotel and chalets had not yet been removed despite his numerous reminders to the Great Northern Railway. Mather was furious. There are varying accounts of what happened, the most colorful being that Mather immediately ordered 13 dynamite sticks to be placed in and around the mill. He then proceeded to call the hotel guests to step outside for the demonstration as he personally ignited the charges in celebration of his daughter's 19th birthday, shouting, "We don't have sawmills in national parks!"

Hill was outraged when he received word of Mather's actions, but he knew the Great Northern had in fact ignored Mather's reminders to remove the mill. He held his anger and ordered his workers to clean up the debris.

MANY GLACIER DINING ROOM WITH GREAT NORTHERN'S ORIENTAL THEME, CIRCA 1920s. Glacier National Park Photo

MANY GLACIER HOTEL, 1920s.
Stan Cohen Collection

One of the most dramatic incidents at the hotel was the Heavens Peak fire of 1936, which started August 19, on the slopes of Heavens Peak. For 12 days 200 acres burned slowly behind park firelines. On the afternoon of August 31, however, strong winds suddenly gusted through the blaze and sent it leaping over the firelines. It didn't take long for the fire to reach Swiftcurrent Pass. At dusk on September 1, the hotel guests saw flames leaping over Swiftcurrent Ridge. With wind funnelling the flame eastward down the valley, the Park Service realized the imminent danger to the hotel and ordered all guests to evacuate the area.

Many of the guests felt the danger was exaggerated and complained as they climbed aboard the buses that would take them to East Glacier. Nevertheless, their exit wasn't a second too soon: flames reached the Many Glacier Chalets just as the buses turned the first corner on the way to Babb.

Hotel employees with shovels, brooms, and buckets joined Park Service workers and began the effort to save the hotel. They hosed down the slate roof and dug trenches encircling the building as the fire gained momentum, quickly roaring its way closer.

Only one hour after it was spotted on Swiftcurrent Pass, the fire had thundered down the valley and engulfed 31 of the Swiftcurrent Motor Inn cabins. Also in its destructive path were Glacier's recently built nature museum and five Many Glacier Chalets. Fortunately, the lake's west shore across from the hotel stopped the main branch of the fire. With less force, the fire divided down both sides of the lake and progressed toward the hotel. As trees ignited along the shore, exploding pine knots shot like flares, often hitting or landing on the hotel building. Using hoses and the plentiful water from the lake, employees sprayed the structure, and drowned the flying embers.

It was truly to the credit of park and hotel employees that the hotel was saved. After several hours, the fire passed. Left behind in the cathedral-like lobby was an exhausted but proud group of workers huddled in blankets and drinking coffee, jubilant at having saved their Many Glacier Hotel.

There is an interesting aside that highlights the ever precarious financial condition of the Glacier Park hotels with their brief, three-month season. The day after the fire, hotel employees sent a triumphant telegram to the Great Northern headquarters in St. Paul. Its exuberant message: "We saved the hotel!" The terse, tongue in cheek reply: "Why?"

MANY GLACIER HOTEL LOBBY WITH CIRCULAR STAIRCASE AND FOUNTAIN. BOTH WERE REMOVED IN 1957 RENOVATIONS TO MAKE ROOM FOR THE GIFT SHOP.

GLADYS MILLHOUSE COMMENTS ON THE LOBBY OF MANY GLACIER HOTEL WITHOUT THE CIRCULAR STAIRCASES. "IT ISN'T AS ROMANTIC NOW. IT WAS REALLY NICE. WE USED TO GO DOWNSTAIRS AND WATCH PLAYS. THEY ALSO HAD DANCES WHILE WE WERE THERE." Glacier National Park Photos

WRANGLERS PACKING SUPPLIES INTO THE BACKCOUNTRY POSSIBLY TO BUILD CHALETS OR TENT CAMPS. Glacier National Park Photo

"BACKED BY THE GREAT NORTHERN, W.J. HILLIGOSS, AN EARLY-DAY PACKER, SET UP A LINE OF TENT CAMPS AT EAST GLACIER, TWO MEDICINE, CUT BANK CREEK, ST. MARY LAKE, GUNSIGHT LAKE AND NEAR THE PRESENT SPERRY CHALETS TO ACCOMMODATE A SADDLE TRIP ACROSS THE PARK." Glacier National Park Photo

CHAPTER FIVE

THE ERA OF THE CHALETS
HAVENS THAT WERE

I shall also, for the convenience of the public...build a number of Swiss Chalets, which would be rented to tourists who prefer to run their own cuisine...the general plan of construction will be the Swiss style of architecture, as this park in time will be known as the Switzerland of America.

W. R. Logan
Park Superintendent, September 1910

*W*hile overseeing the building of Glacier Park Lodge and Many Glacier Hotel, Louis W. Hill also directed construction of chalets situated throughout the park. While Belton Chalet was accessible by auto or train, the eight backcountry chalets were connected by water or trail for boats, hikers and horsemen. These chalets catered to visitors who would spend a week or two touring the park, experiencing its pristine wilderness, and at the same time enjoying the comforts of a warm meal and sheltered sleep.

In the park's early years, dirt roads connected the lodges. Automobile trips were bumpy and slow, especially when tires blew on jagged rocks and engines overheated on steep slopes. Without the Going-to-the-Sun Road, which wasn't completed for through traffic until 1932, it was impossible to see the splendors in the heart of the park by auto. Therefore, the most frequent and popular way to see the vastness of Glacier was by guided horse trips. In 1925 there were over 1,000 horses in the park and over 10,000 tourists enjoying horse tours. Because the difficult travel did not allow freedom to tour the park in even a few hours as we can today, visitors came to Glacier with a commitment to extended stays in order to experience the park's trails, campfire coffee, storytelling and mountain views of sun and storm.

Former Lake McDonald area resident Cora Hutchings recalls, "The trips would take most of the day and usually the guides would have a certain place established for the noon lunch; they would have their own coffeepots, fireplaces and box lunches." Visitors of the 1920s and '30s often experienced 10- to 14-day tours through Glacier's backcountry.

Louis W. Hill designed the trail and chalet network carefully. In various places tent camps were interspersed along the 10 to 18 miles of trail that connected each chalet with the next chalet. Not only were the pack trips adventuresome for the visitors, but they also relieved pressure from the popular main lodges, which were overflowing with guests.

The hotels and chalets were closed during World War I and for three seasons between 1942 and 1945 during World War II. The hotels were able to recover from the lack of use and upkeep, while some of the chalets suffered irreparably. St. Mary, Cutbank, and Going-to-the-Sun Chalets were all razed between 1944 and

1949, with those at Two Medicine falling in 1953, ending an era for most of Glacier National Park's backcountry chalets. Granite Park Chalet, 7.5 miles from Logan Pass on the Highline Trail, and Sperry Chalet, 6.5 miles up from Lake McDonald, closed in 1993 for renovation and have since reopened with further work planned as funding permits.

BELTON CHALET

In the early 1890s, during the Great Northern's construction days, the crew's camp at the west entrance of Glacier National Park was named after Daniel Webster Bell. Over time, the "Bell Town" camp grew and evolved into the town of Belton.

The Belton Chalet stands directly outside the park boundary in present-day West Glacier. Because the railroad stopped at the west entrance to the park, lodging was a necessity, and the Belton Chalet primarily served passengers of the Great Northern.

Former Belton resident Gonhilde "Bud" Henderson worked as a dispatcher at the Belton Depot from 1917 to 1927. She remembers the town's early days:

"The Belton Chalet was built in 1910-1911 and people don't appreciate the effort of building them at that time...The train depot was the center of the town's activity in those days, especially in the summer, as visitors arrived for their stay in Glacier Park. Between the depot [which used to stand closer to the chalet, but has since been moved west from its original location] and the Belton Chalet, there was a pagoda covered with Virginia Creeper vines, which enclosed the path between the depot and the chalet's office." Now, Highway 2 runs between the depot and the chalet, greatly changing the original chalet and depot layout.

Many anecdotes accompany the hotel business, and Bud recalls one incident at the Belton Chalet: "The chalet had a Swiss gardener named Hauser who came each summer for several years from Menominee, Wisconsin. Mr. Hauser was an excellent gardener and kept the grounds around the area beautifully trimmed. There was a hedge all along the wall by the railroad tracks and many varieties of trees grew on the well-kept lawns. One man stepped off the train and asked, 'Is this Glacier Park?'" When Bud replied that it was, the man said, "Why, it's not as big as Manitou City Park in Spokane!" He had mistaken the grounds in front of the Belton depot and chalet for the entire Glacier National Park!

Today, the Belton Chalet buildings are privately owned by Andy Baxter and Cas Still. After three years of restoration, the 1999 season marked the reopening of the Belton Chalet. For the first time in over 50 years, the main lodge, chalet, cabins and restaurant are now in full operation. Unlike other historic lodgings in the park, the Belton Chalet, located at West Glacier, can open earlier in the spring and stay open later in the fall. The Belton Chalet is on the National Register of Historic Places and has been nominated as a National Historic Landmark.

REMEMBERING CHALETS PAST

The eight backcountry chalets received most of their business from the guided horse tours. Many of these trips started from East Glacier. Travelers riding the park's eastern route would leave from Glacier Park Lodge on the "Outside Trail," then ride to Two Medicine Chalet, Cutbank Chalet and on to St. Mary Chalets. From there they would head west to Going-to-the-Sun Chalets. After a night or two in those classy accommodations, they had two options. They could venture north over Piegan Pass to the Many Glacier Chalet and Hotel and continue to Granite Park Chalet and Waterton Lake. This was part of the "North Circle" tour. Another option was the "Inside Trail" which took them to Gunsight Lake and over Lincoln Pass to Sperry Chalet. After about two weeks or so on the trail, they would arrive at Lewis Glacier Hotel at Lake McDonald. At the hotel they would be warmly greeted and their luggage, having been shipped from East Glacier, would await them. The riders would be more than ready to shed their smoke-scented riding clothes and slip into dancing attire for evenings of music and entertainment.

BELTON CHALET IN ITS EARLY DAYS. CIRCA 1915. Glacier National Park Photo

TWO MEDICINE CHALET

The Great Northern began constructing the chalet network on the east side of the park beginning with the Two Medicine Chalet in 1911. The chalet was set on the east shore of Two Medicine Lake, 12 miles north of Glacier Park Lodge. Used by guided horse tours, it became the first overnight stop on the "Outside Trail" tour. By 1914 the chalet was complete, with a dining hall and dormitory.

Helene Dawson Edkins, of the first family in Midvale (now East Glacier), remembers the Two Medicine Chalet: "...Dad built the chalet at Two Medicine, which is now standing...He built a number of the little buildings at Two Medicine, which have been taken down, but the chalet, the present chalet, was one that he built. I used to go up there while he was building it."

The highlights of fame that the Two Medicine Chalet boasts are visits by two former presidents of the United States. In August 1930, use of the Two Medicine Chalet was set aside for President Hoover and his party. The chalet was deemed the "Summer White House." Then, in 1934, President Franklin D. Roosevelt stayed for two days at the chalet during his "National Parks Year" tour. From the chalet, Roosevelt broadcast a "Fireside Chat" speech in which he spoke on our national parks:

"Today, for the first time in my life, I have seen Glacier Park. Perhaps I can best express to you my thrill and delight by saying that I wish every American, old and young, could have been with me today. The great mountains, the glaciers, the lakes

TWO MEDICINE CHALET, POST CARD VIEW. From an original post card

and the trees make me long to stay here for all the rest of the summer...There is nothing so American as our national parks." Roosevelt had quite a warm reception with powwows and entertainment provided by the park's Civilian Conservation Corps (CCC). He was also inducted into the Blackfeet tribe and gained the name "Big Chief."

The Two Medicine Chalet was closed in 1942 due to World War II and did not reopen until after the war. Unfortunately, the cabins and dormitory fell into disrepair and were torn down. Tom Dawson, who helped build the Two Medicine Chalet structures, also had the contract of dismantling them. In the winter of 1953, workers removed all but the main dining hall, which was later converted into the present camp store.

The Two Medicine Camp Store is now on the National Register of Historic Places.

CUTBANK CHALET

The Cutbank Chalet was tucked in a niche of scenery on the east side of the park, 18 miles north of the Two Medicine Chalet.

The horse tours travelled from East Glacier to Two Medicine, from Two Medicine to Cutbank, from Cutbank to Red Eagle and from Red Eagle to St. Mary. "It made a lovely four-day trip," according to early park employee Mrs. Merlin Staples, "and they called it the 'Outside Trail.'"

The Cutbank Chalet had an irregular operating record. It was the easiest chalet to close from season to season if the tourist travel to the park was less promising than other years, but its closure disrupted the trail trip from East Glacier through to St. Mary. The Cutbank Chalet was closed during World Wars I and II, fell into disrepair and with many of the other chalets was razed by 1949.

ST. MARY CHALETS

Centered between Glacier Park Lodge and Many Glacier Hotel, at the junction of the East Entrance to the park, St. Mary Chalets were used mostly as a transfer point for travellers. The chalets catered to a crowd that dropped in for the day, maybe just for a meal and sometimes overnight, but not usually for an extended stay. The chalets had a higher turnover, sending guests west to Going-to-the-Sun Chalets, north to Many Glacier Hotel or south to Glacier Park Lodge. The chalets were built on St. Mary Lake and had boat service for guests, shuttling them to the Going-to-the-Sun Chalets, about eight miles by water.

George E. Ferguson, assistant porter at the chalets, remembers his first days there in 1923: "On arrival at the Glacier Park Station on that June day, we of the St. Mary staff were given food and lodging at the big 'entrance' hotel and the next day taken by bus to St. Mary Chalets. The first few days of each season were devoted to the strenuous task of 'opening up' in time that facilities were available for the

CUT BANK CHALET, CIRCA 1912. UM Archives

THIS ST. MARY CHALET WAS A VERY ELABORATE BUILDING WITH A HUGE STONE FIREPLACE. Glacier
National Park Photo

St. Mary Lake 1912

Eighteen miles from the Cut Bank colony on the Lower End of Upper St. Mary Lake, the third group of chalets is being constructed. Lower St. Mary is one of the most beautiful in the entire park and also one of the largest. Nine buildings are being constructed here—one 18 by 60 feet log chalet club room, dining room and kitchen, two two-story log chalets 28 by 28 feet and six one-story chalets 18 by 18 feet. Accommodations for 100 people. Glacier National Park Photo

earliest tourists. This first called for a clean-up of the main lodge, especially the kitchen and dining room—often beginning with the eviction of winter tenants in the form of animal life and the removal of mortar 'chinking' that had fallen from between the logs used in the construction of the outside walls in all of the buildings."

Following their closure during World War II, the St. Mary Chalets were torn down in 1944.

GOING-TO-THE-SUN CHALETS

When one stands at Sun Point, it is difficult to imagine the former hustle and bustle encompassing nine buildings on this rocky peninsula. Sheer cliffs rise to the east and the western panorama of Citadel, Little Chief and Going-to-the-Sun mountains is prominent against St. Mary Lake's deep blue hue. Along the hillside, chunks of concrete are strewn down the bank. The rubble of rock and cement pillars tells of three support foundations that once stood strong across the hill. In your mind construct the rest of the chalet, imagining an amazingly beautiful building of log and stone set against the peaks. Some of the buildings perched high on the ledge and all nestled on a sloping rock slab some 100 feet above the lake. Going-to-the-Sun Chalets were the showiest of the chalets, and the most centrally located—accessible by trail, boat and eventually by auto, with the construction of Going-to-the-Sun Road. The buildings consisted of a dining room, eight chalets for guest sleeping quarters, and dorms for employees.

Former employee Mrs. Herbert Johnson recalls, "I was only 18 the summer of 1923 when I was a waitress at St. Mary Chalets and only 19 the summer of 1924, which I spent as a waitress at Going-to-the-Sun Chalets. To reach Going-to-the-Sun we had to take the boat from St. Mary Chalets. We could go by trail on horseback or on foot, but the road between the two chalets was not yet built. In spite of the distance between the two chalets we had record crowds at Going-to-the-Sun."

Now strewn about on the ground, one finds "Thomas" porcelain bases for the electric wiring, glass chips from windows and jars, even pieces of a saucer and a small section of blue willow china. A broken brick reads "Evens & Ho...St. Louis." Memories among the rubble speak of late nights on the front deck-a brilliant sunset sparked with wine and laughter, the boat sidling to the dock with a new group of boarders, and waitresses dressed in their Swiss uniforms, welcoming visitors to the Sun Point haven.

The chalets, built in 1913, served the park until 1940. They were closed during WWI and WWII. Never reopened after WWII, these buildings were razed in 1949. In their short 27 year history they were a well loved link in the chalet experience.

"I felt very bad when my husband and I drove out through Glacier Park about 12 years ago [in 1967] to find that St. Mary Chalets were completely gone," Mrs.

GOING-TO-THE-SUN CHALETS

Two views of the Going-to-the-Sun Chalets which sat on the shores of St. Mary Lake at the eastern end of the park. Glacier National Park Photo

"Sun Chalets Removed by Park Service

Glacier National Park's well-known Going-to-the-Sun Chalets are no more. Workmen have just completed removing the last logs of the Swiss type encampment that was at the narrows on St. Mary lake. The chalets had not been used since before the war, and were beyond economical repair. *Great Falls Tribune*, 1949. Glacier National Park Photo

"CAP SWANSON OPERATED THE LAUNCH THAT RAN ON THE LAKE BETWEEN ST. MARY AND GOING-TO-THE-SUN CHALETS. THERE WAS NO ROAD BETWEEN THESE POINTS AT THIS TIME, JUST A HORSE TRAIL ALONG THE LAKE." EVA BEEBE. Glacier National Park Photo

WAITRESSES AT GOING-TO-THE-SUN CHALETS WERE OUTFITTED TO GIVE A EUROPEAN LOOK TO THE SETTING. Glacier National Park Photo

Johnson remembers. "The only thing left was the old dock on St. Mary Lake. We also drove up to Going-to-the-Sun Chalets to discover that all those beautiful buildings were gone. I have often wondered if the buildings were in such bad shape that they could not be repaired. To my young eyes they were beautiful."

GUNSIGHT CHALET

Gunsight Chalet was located at the foot of Gunsight Lake for only a few brief seasons. Unfortunately, it is difficult to discern the exact year it was destroyed. The Superintendent's Report of 1913 lists Gunsight Chalet with a dining room and dormitory, but no mention is made of it in future annual reports. It is believed that in the winter of 1913-1914, an avalanche roared down the adjacent mountain and swept over the chalet, destroying its humble beginnings and proving its lake-shore location a risky proposition. There was an attempt to keep a tent-like structure as the chalet, but, according to former Director of the National Park Service, Horace Albright, the Gunsight tent structure was destroyed by a bear in 1915. There is no mention of an attempt to relocate the Gunsight Chalet, and its history is fleeting.

An excerpt in Mary Robert Rinehart's book, *Through Glacier Park*, captures one memory of the chalet: "There was some grunting when at the end of that day we fell out of our saddles, but no one complaining. That night, for the first time, the Eaton Party (42 with Charlie Russell) slept under a roof at the Gunsight Chalet, on the shores of a blue lake."

The following day the group continued over Gunsight and Lincoln Pass to Sperry camp. The last day of the trip ushered the group to the west-side trailhead near the Lewis Glacier Hotel (now Lake McDonald Lodge) for an evening of dining and dancing.

MANY GLACIER CHALET

The Many Glacier Chalet structures preceded Many Glacier Hotel by one year. The eight chalet cabins were built on the southwest slope of Mount Altyn in 1913, and overlooked the site of the future hotel. These chalets were the northern-most chalets and were part of the North Circle tour. There were eight chalets in all.

Five of the chalet cabins were destroyed in the 1936 Heavens Peak fire that swept down the valley from Swiftcurrent Pass. Chalet "C" was destroyed by an avalanche from Mount Altyn, and the remaining two, situated near Swiftcurrent Falls at the outlet of Swiftcurrent Lake, are still in use by maintenance personnel.

***

After traveling by horseback for days on end, the sight of a welcoming chalet was undoubtedly a delight. With soft beds and fresh linen, a dining-room dinner, drinks and clean clothes, the chalets and hotels offered trail-weary travelers a refuge of luxury amidst the rigors of "roughing it" in the wilderness.

GUNSIGHT LAKE CHALET. Montana Historical Society

A MANY GLACIER CHALET WITH MOUNT WILBUR IN THE BACKGROUND. Glacier National Park Photo

GRANITE PARK CHALET. Glacier National Park Photo

"ON LINE—GLACIER NATIONAL PARK, JULY 24, 1915
MR. T.D. MCMAHON:
BE SURE AND GET THE LUMBER OUT FOR THE PACK HORSES TO TAKE TO FINISH GRANITE PARK. WE WANT TO RUSH THIS TO COMPLETION AND HAVE NO FURTHER DELAY. L.W. HILL" Glacier National Park Photo

CHAPTER SIX

GRANITE PARK AND SPERRY CHALETS
HALLMARKS OF HISTORY

Sperry Chalet and luncheon. No more the ham and coffee over a wood fire, the cutting of much bread on a flat stone. Here were tables, chairs and linen. Alas, there was a waitress who crumbed the table and brought in dessert.

Mary Roberts Rinehart
Through Glacier Park, 1916

*G*ranite Park and Sperry Chalets are the last remaining hope of preserving the memory of the chalet era in Glacier National Park. Up until the summer of 1993, they were the only two remaining chalets that operated as the chalets were originally designed. They accommodated overnight guests, providing them with food and lodging in a cozy, but rustic, wilderness setting. The chalets were also a welcome sight to day hikers, who would drop in for homemade pie and coffee and a short rest before hitting the trail again.

In autumn 1992, Granite Park and Sperry Chalets were closed by the National Park Service because they failed to meet current standards set forth by Congress in the Clean Water Act and the Safe Drinking Water Act. Following renovations, in 1996 Granite Park Chalet was reopened for the present as a hiker's shelter, while Sperry Chalet reopened with traditional services in 1999.

These mountain refuges are set six to eight miles from the Going-to-the-Sun Road and are accessible only by trail. Originally, they were part of the eight chalet system that tourists visited as they linked their trip from chalet to chalet. In the early days, when there was no transmountain road through the park, the railroad established tent camps between the chalet stops to bridge the long distances. The unique feature of the Sperry and Granite Park Chalets, which sets them apart from the other chalets, is their construction of stone quarried from the building site. Their solid construction is one reason the buildings have withstood years of severe Glacier winters.

The chalets have been through both happy and rough times as changes in and around Glacier National Park have progressed. The most prosperous time for the chalets, however, has been under the leadership of Ross and Kay Luding and their extended family.

Kay recalls, "I had read a little story in *The Hungry Horse News* and thought about it. 'Wouldn't that be great for the kids? Ross likes to cook. I like to be around people. I like the idea of a hotel/motel and the kids are just the right age to break in.'"

After a chance meeting with Superintendent John W. Emmert at a 1954 Mother's Day picnic in the park, Ross and Kay Luding were launched into a job that would drastically change their lives. The Ludings gained the title of concessioner that season. For the following season—and for the next 39 years—the family committed their summers to running the chalets.

Kay recalls her first day at Sperry Chalet. It was July 10, but still spring in the highcountry: The snow was so bad that when we went in at Sperry we had to shovel steps down to the front door to get in there. It was a nice warm day, I remember that! Oh, we had a ball! The rats were in everything. As I walked into the dining room, the shutters were still on all but one window. There was just enough light to see several rats nests between every shutter on all those windows.

Since the sleeping quarters were minimal and the chalets had a small staff, the Ludings agreed to operate both chalets similarly, hiring only female employees. Although working in a backcountry chalet sounds glamorous, the work schedule was more rigorous and demanding than town jobs. Plus, there was little time off.

Most of the Luding family worked there, with Ross as manager at Sperry Chalet, Kay as headmother, their children Barbara, and Lanny, and Kay's sister and two nieces all pitching in various summers. It was truly a family affair, and the chalets provided some of their richest times, according to Kay.

We put the kids to work. They could do the work very well. My sister [Marge] came along for the leadership. She took care of the hotel and she had two little daughters. The youngest was four years old, the other was nine—and between Barbara, Connie, Beth and Marcia, who was the little errand girl, everybody worked. Lanny helped with laundry and was a nice handyman around there and Ross kept running up and down the hill to get the groceries. Ross only worked at Sperry as a cook that one summer. I can't say I learned to cook from him, but I got stuck with the job!

In 1955, during the Ludings' second season as concessioner, they opened Granite Park Chalet. While Kay stayed devoted to Sperry, Ross spent most of his summers at Granite Park. As numerous miles separate the two chalets, Ross and Kay arranged special dates throughout the summers to see each other:

Those were the most joyous times we had together as husband and wife. I'd be working at Sperry and we'd be on the radio and we'd plan an event. So I'd start running off the hill from Sperry—start out the door with a bang and start running all the way down and I'd be down by 5:00 p.m. and we'd go out to dinner together, maybe at the hotel. Then we'd go up to the Loop and start hiking. And we'd be [at Granite Park Chalet] by the 9:00 p.m. coffee hour. Sometimes we didn't tell them we were coming and so I'd help carry the load and we'd have ice cream wrapped in dry ice and Ross would take pop in his backpack for the kids. They didn't get much of that kind of stuff and it was kind of a treat for them. It was like Christmas. We had a lot of gay times together going up there like that. Those were the times I remember best as being the most fun. It was hard work going in and out but it sure toughened me up.

The girls at Granite Park had a more difficult time getting off the mountain on

their days off. Since it was eight miles down Swiftcurrent Pass to the Many Glacier Valley, and about the same distance to the Going-to-the-Sun Road, they were more isolated. The kids would want to go and Ross would say, 'No, it's too far!' That's 16 miles in a day! That's a lot of footwork! It was really tough so we didn't put laws on those kids over there. We said do what you can. Most of those girls were hikers and they'd hike the seven miles there and back in a day from the Highline Trail. They took turns and it took them all summer to get broken into that. They finally got to where they could hike down to Swiftcurrent Campground and right back up again in a short period of time. They had a different kind of entertainment.

Working at the chalets was a job, but it also created a small-family feeling among the workers. Kay and Ross did their best to make the summer unique and unforgettable for the girls:

We had a lot of fun-we made everything fun. We had days where nobody would show up because we didn't have reservations when we started. Sometimes there were two or three days in a row where not a soul came up that hill and if the weather was bad it was all ours. We just simply had fun. We had an old phonograph there [and two records]. They wore it out, in fact, and they danced in there and pretended. They had a marvelous time!

The evenings were the girls' time off and they cherished the socializing and coffee hours. We had so many kinds of people every night, and they all had their own questions. And when a ranger was there it was far more excitement. Particularly on the days Doug Follet walked in. He was the center of amusement to everybody and he will always be that way. He's at his very best when he's standing in the center of a bunch of people making wisecracks. But the nights Doug and I got together it was hilarious. It was just outright hilarious. There was so much to talk about-so much to tease about. We had so darn much fun!

Coffee hour was always special. One of us kids was responsible for coffee hour each night. In other words if I had coffee hour I had to see to it that the coffee was made, the cups and saucers were out and everything that was needed was there and if we had any extra cookies they got them. Usually they were gone because the cookies went like everything. Like snow in July.

Ross Luding died in March 1979, leaving Kay and family with both chalets. Kay continued as headmother of Sperry and her son Lanny took over his father's position as overall administrator of Belton Chalets, Incorporated.

On September 1, 1983, through the organizational efforts of Mike Olinger, the National Park Service celebrated "K" Day, honoring Kay Luding for 30 years of outstanding service in continual operation of Sperry and Granite Park Chalets. Her total devotion as headmother made the chalets ring with praise from the guests.

All that it adds up to are the letters that I've gotten, Kay said. They all say the same thing. The same sentence I hear over and over again in letters year after year piled on top: 'It was the most wonderful thing I've ever done for myself,' or

'It was the highlight of my whole life.' And I get to thinking, 'Wow.' It's a once-in-a-lifetime experience to go to either place.

I think it was said best by one little eight-year-old girl. She had already come to the chalet and she had already been to Sperry Glacier and she took the trip over to Lake Ellen Wilson before they went down, and she told her mom, 'Mother, my eyes simply can't take anymore.' And I thought what a beautiful way to put it: 'My cup runneth over.' I was so thrilled when I heard that! That's why we write back and forth today; that's why I have such a wonderful audience today.

The Luding family has a wealth of memories of Granite Park and Sperry Chalets, as do all of us who have visited Glacier National Park and Glacier's grandest buildings. With the continued efforts to open both the chalets to traditional service, Granite and Sperry Chalets will provide future visitors with their own heritage of memories.

* * * * *

Currently The Glacier Fund raises money for projects like the chalets as well as other important renovations in Glacier National Park. If you would like to contribute to this fund please contact the National Park Foundation—The Glacier Fund, 1101 - 17th St. NW Suite 1102, Washington, DC 20036 or call 1-888-434-9330. (Specify: Save The Chalets Fund).

Granite Park Chalet is now open, temporarily, as a hiker's shelter, and Sperry Chalet has reopened with traditional guest services thanks to the collaborative efforts of numerous volunteers, Save the Chalets Foundation and the National Park Service.

Granite Park and Sperry Chalets are designated National Historic Landmarks.

SPERRY CHALET. NOTICE THE GREAT NORTHERN RAILWAY SIGNATURE ON THE END OF THE BUILDING. Glacier National Park Photo

THE ELEGANT PRINCE OF WALES HOTEL ON WATERTON LAKE, ALBERTA, CANADA. Glacier National Park Photo

INTERIOR VIEW OF THE PRINCE OF WALES HOTEL. Glacier National Park Photo

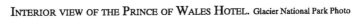

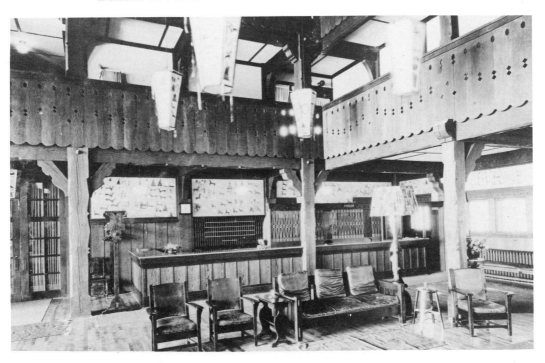

CHAPTER SEVEN

PRINCE OF WALES HOTEL
THE ELEGANT CANADIAN

Waterton National Park is the Canadian counterpart of Glacier National Park in Northern Montana. The two lie side by side on the International boundary. Boundary posts dot the boundary line; the American flag on one, the Union Jack on the other!

Lethbridge Herald
1926

*I*t is mentioned in *The Diary of Kootenai Brown* that in September of 1913, Louis W. Hill ventured from St. Paul to Glacier National Park by rail, most likely transporting his personal automobile as well. On this trip, Hill motored up the newly constructed road to Waterton and reaffirmed his dream to build a fourth lodge on the crest overlooking Waterton Lake and townsite.

Although Hill's idea to build a Canadian counterpart hotel originated simultaneously with building the Montana hotels, the Prince of Wales Hotel was not begun until 1927, fifteen years after Glacier National Park's accommodations were completed.

According to Ray Djuff in *The Prince of Wales Hotel*, there were several good reasons for the delay in building the Prince of Wales. First, World War I began in 1914. While the United States was not initially involved, Canada was at war immediately. Therefore, Canada could not place a high priority on domestic concerns such as new buildings in her national parks, and Hill's Waterton hotel was put on hold. Following World War I, another obstacle prevented Hill from building the Prince of Wales Hotel: there was a heated controversy in Waterton regarding the building of a dam between the upper and lower Waterton Lakes. This distraction again stalled the project as no leases were issued for the area while the debate continued.

Djuff notes, interestingly, that Prohibition was in effect in the United States in the early 1920s and it has been said that perhaps the Great Northern Railway saw the potential of Waterton as a way to lure Americans across the border. Whatever the reasons for building the hotel, whether to attract business or to bring the two parks closer together in international friendship, Hill continued to believe his Canadian hotel should be built.

By 1926 Louis W. Hill was ready to finalize the hotel plans. When rumor surfaced that Hill would be returning to Waterton to make the final arrangements, the *Lethbridge Herald* stated, "It bodes well for the future of Waterton Park that the chief executive of the Great Northern is taking a keen, decided and personal interest in the new hotel here."

And so the Prince of Wales was built at Waterton. In 1926, the Great Northern

Railway contracted with Canadian builders Doug Oland and Jim Scott for the project. Oland and Scott had just completed a beautifully designed and crafted dance hall in Waterton in 1925 which established a respectable name for them, thus setting the stage for the Great Northern's choice of builders.

The *Prince of Wales Hotel* mentions that Oland and Scott faced many delays as they struggled to meet the one-year deadline. First, numerous rainy days in autumn turned the dirt roads into mud, forcing the workers to haul supplies by horse and wagon rather than by truck. Also, the wind on the knoll is fierce and the hotel is unprotected from forceful gusts. Strong winds blew lumber about the site on more than one occasion and before the builders could stabilize the building, it was blown out of alignment. With all of the delays, winter arrived before the new hotel was enclosed causing further obstacles and expenses with blowing and drifting snow.

Also, Louis W. Hill was still revising the hotel's blueprints. Even after the foundation concrete was poured, Hill altered the structural design of the building numerous times. For example, the hotel originally was to be similar in design to the Many Glacier Hotel in Montana, but with 62 additional rooms. During the course of the year, Hill reduced this number by more than three-fourths, changing the original building plans from 300 to a minimal 65 rooms. Also, instead of the original low, horizontal four-story structure, Hill dramatically changed his plans, modeling the hotel instead as a seven-story European chalet with dormer windows and steep, gabled roofs.

Even though Hill made extensive alterations to the hotel's blueprints, he would not change the July 7, 1927, construction deadline. According to Djuff, in order to stay on the strict schedule, Oland and Scott received permission from the federal government to work on Sundays and expand their work force from 60 men in January to 230 men by June 1927.

Despite Oland and Scott's valiant efforts to open in early July, the builders were unable to meet the deadline and the Prince of Wales Hotel opened 18 days after Hill planned, on July 25, 1927.

Unlike Glacier Park Lodge's grand opening, the Prince of Wales Hotel celebrated a quiet first evening. Djuff describes a small dinner honoring Oland and Scott. There were 172 for dinner that night with a house count of 80 registered guests.

When the bill to establish Glacier as a national park was before Congress in 1910, U.S. Senator Penrose stated with insight : 'This park will be international in character.' Following his prediction the Rotary Clubs of Alberta, Canada and Montana met in 1931 and proposed joining the two parks to create a single Waterton-Glacier International Peace Park. The proposal gained wide public and legislative support and by 1932 President Hoover and the Canadian Parliament signed the bill into law.

The Prince of Wales Hotel's ownership has always stayed connected with the Glacier National Park concessions although the hotel is well within the Canadian border. Because the hotel operates as a business ultimately responsible to the Canadian government, it is in some ways run by a separate set of rules from the Glacier National Park hotels. For example, a U.S. Citizen can work at the Prince of Wales Hotel, but only with special permission. Joint U.S.-Canadian administration can present special challenges.

Nevertheless, overlooking Waterton Lake stands the regal Prince of Wales Hotel, remaining to this day the most visible reminder of the symbolic unity of the Waterton-Glacier International Peace Park.

THE LARGE WINDOWS IN THE PRINCE OF WALES HOTEL LOOK OUT ON BEAUTIFUL WATERTON LAKE.
Stan Cohen Collection

"It came with somewhat of a pleasant shock to the people of Canada last spring when President Ralph Budd of the Great Northern Railway system announced in New York plans for the establishment of a million dollar hotel in the Canadian Rockies at Waterton National Park.

Lethbridge Herald, 1926

Swift Current Motor Inn's store and coffee shop after remodeling, September 1956.
Glacier National Park Photo

General store and lunch room of Rising Sun Motor Inn, June 1941. Glacier National Park Photo

CHAPTER EIGHT

MOTOR INNS
TRAVELLERS' RESPITE

In the aftermath of the 1929 stock market crash, Americans began to discover that they could no longer afford all-expense tours of the park sponsored by the railway.... Indeed, there was a new and growing concern for the ability of Glacier's tourist facilities to supply the wants of a mobile, motor-borne vacationer. The winds of progress were now blowing strongly enough to mask the whistles of the Great Northern's passenger trains.

Michael Ober
Enmity and Alliance...1973

*W*hen most travel to Glacier transferred from railway to automobile, visitor numbers soared, annually setting new records. Park travel increased dramatically as the auto became favored for touring. Auto travel also demanded a transmountain route through the park and by July 1933, the completion of the Going-to-the-Sun Road attracted even more sightseers. The increase in visitors made lodging demands on the park that the main hotels could not fulfill. Also, with the introduction of the automobile, Glacier became less of a haven for the well-to-do and more a park for all people. The park's main hotels were too expensive for tourists just looking to visit Glacier over the weekend, so they ventured outside the park to find lodging. The National Park Service recognized the public's need for affordable accommodations within the park and encouraged the Great Northern's Glacier Park Hotel Company to construct motor inns.

At first, the company stalled on its decision. It was difficult for the railroad to acknowledge the end of an era of rail travel. With auto travelers outnumbering rail passenger arrivals to the park, the Great Northern's profits were low. Now the railroad was being asked to support America's newest travel trend and ultimately, the railroad's competitor.

Eventually, the Great Northern saw the potential in additional lodging in Glacier and built two motor inns over a 10-year period. In 1930, starting with a few cabins, Swiftcurrent Motor Inn was built about a mile west of Many Glacier Hotel. By 1934, the motor inn had proved successful and the Great Northern added 45 more cabins. Tragically, Swiftcurrent Motor Inn lost all but 12 of its cabins in the Heavens Peak fire of 1936.

The second inn to be built was Roes Creek Inn (now Rising Sun). Set 6 miles into the park from the St. Mary entrance on the Going-to-the-Sun Road. Rising Sun Motor Inn opened June 15, 1940.

After 1952 the Village Inn on the west side of the park helped alleviate the lodging needs in the Lake McDonald area. The Inn sits at the foot of Lake McDonald in Apgar, with a spectacular view across the lake.

The motor inns are more casual than the main hotels and are family oriented with motel units, cabins, campstores and cafes. These accommodations as well as the park's campgrounds help fulfill the promise of Congress' act to establish Glacier as a national park in 1910 which stated that Glacier National Park should be a "pleasure ground for the benefit and enjoyment of the people."

"When I was up there—about 10 years ago—I tried to tell one of the drivers, 'These buses were old in 1947!' He looked at me as if I was crazy. They were just keeping those buses going, replacing parts of them. I remember they steam cleaned the engines—that was a big deal. They really took care of them." Trudi Carleton Peek. Glacier National Park Photo

CHAPTER NINE
THE RED BUS FLEET
A WHEELED REVERIE

Glacier National Park is the finest of all places and it's our privilege to give our Red Bus riders their best possible experience of the park.

Joe Kendall
Red Bus driver, September 1999

*C*amaraderie. That's the Red Bus byword. Each Red Bus passenger group bands together in concert, while the driver as maestro orchestrates their tour of Glacier National Park. The Red Buses ply the park byways between Many Glacier, East Glacier and Lake McDonald as well as the Going-to-the-Sun road, providing narrated tours for viewing, photography and quiet wonderment. Also the Red Buses provide shuttle services for the East and West Glacier Amtrak train stations and Glacier International Airport as well as hikers and park employees.

Red Bus driver, or "gear jammer," Joe Kendall spins tales of the Red Bus fleet, thought to be the oldest continuous transportation enterprise in the world. The Glacier Park Bus service began in 1914 and was upgraded in the 1930s with White Motor Company buses. Those 1930s Red Buses, each with an oak and sheet metal body on a White Motor Company chassis, operated until 1999 when the Ford Motor Company generously upgraded the fleet.

Joe Kendall, at this writing a Glacier Park Red Bus gear jammer in the summer, operates an Illinois farm in the winter. With energies that belie their years, Joe and his wife, Geri have enjoyed their summer jobs in Glacier National Park. Fifty years ago, before he was married, Joe had worked as a dishwasher at Lake McDonald Lodge.

Joe Kendall says that conversion of the gearshift Red Buses to automatic transmissions in 1989, made him and his 40 fellow tour drivers "shiftless gear jammers." All Red Bus drivers dispense information with humor–"To tell the difference between ravens and crows, observe whether there are two, or three pinion feathers on the wings–it's a matter of opinion." Or the woman Red Bus driver with a group of rather serious passengers from the Netherlands who asked what to do when a bear is seen. "Form a circle around me," she replied, uncertain whether her joke was appreciated. She was soon reassured on this point when a distant bear wandered into view and her passengers, all in smiles, did indeed encircle their guide.

Joe Kendall describes, in the early days of the Red Buses, an esprit de corps among drivers, who had the best jobs in the park and a girl friend at every stop. The "college man" drivers with law, medical, engineering, etc., careers ahead of them were an elite corps, who over the years have continued an outstanding safety record.

The gear jammers' camaraderie is attested by a recent 50-year reunion where great stories abounded, including the bus "Super" who was a stickler that at day's end, each Red Bus be washed and buffed to a shine. One day, several parked buses were scratched by an airplane's tail as a truck carried the aircraft in sections over Logan Pass. Imagine the Supervisor's consternation as each driver explained the scratch on his bus, "an airplane clipped me going over Logan Pass."

The Red Buses of Glacier National Park embody living history. With the 1910 establishment of the park, early roads were muddy and chuckholed so that horsedrawn 11 passenger coaches owned by Brewster Brothers of Canada drove the wagon roads from Glacier Park Station trains at East Glacier into the Two Medicine, Cutbank, St. Mary and Many Glacier valleys.

Glacier Park Transport Company owner, Montana native Roe Emery, brought in White Motor Company buses in 1914, the first motor transport in any national park. Horses remained important, as eight-horse teams hitched to the front axles would pull the buses through hub high mudholes, with the teamsters riding the front fenders.

Glacier National Park roads were gradually paved and by 1930, 60 convertible "ragtop" roadsters had replaced the early fleet. From 1936 to 1939, thirty-three 18 passenger White Motor Company Red Buses replaced the previous "ragtops." By dint of careful maintenance, these "new" buses have operated until the present day.

In 1999 at Lake McDonald Lodge, right after discharging its passengers, a Red Bus chassis settled to the pavement when its metal frame failed. On investigation Amy Vanderbilt's Red Bus Team advised overhauling the entire fleet. Dennis Schwecke, a Ford employee and Montana native, along with Red Bus chief mechanic Larry Hegg, outlined Red Bus needs to Bill Ford, who brought the Ford Motor Company aboard as a Glacier Park "proud partner." Two years of extra work hours, often donated by Schwecke and hundreds of others ensued. By 2002 in a June snowstorm, East Glacier welcomed 20 refurbished Red Buses back from Michigan. Soon Ford had the entire Red Bus Fleet in service with restored bodies, new power trains and low emission propane engines, each on a new Ford E-450 chassis stretched to the original White Motor Company wheelbase.

The buses retain the romantic 1930s design of the Count Alexis de Sakhoffsky continental European exterior, so that our history becomes the future. As many parks and adjoining regions evaluate transportation options, Glacier Park spokeswoman Amy Vanderbilt asks whether the Red Bus idea might inspire other parks. With retro all the rage, it could happen.

REPRISE

*T*he breezes of Glacier whisper along the timbered shores of Lake McDonald and push and pull the cedars. The water at mid-lake is caught and rolls forward, rippling and splashing toward the shore. The rhythm of the wind sends waves that break and fall back against the next wave, over the pebbled beach.

Past the rocky lake shore, the wind lifts and throws its strength against the Garden Wall. There the rock is unmoved by the wind, whose force whips around the massif and funnels up the wall to the top, where it surges eastward, over the foothills and beyond.

Here, nestled by lakes and forests, tucked into valleys of awe-inspiring scenery, stand four great lodges. At one time, nine chalets also stood in this place, and while only some of the lodges and chalets were connected by road, all were accessible by trail and travelers came by the thousands to experience Glacier.

From the westbound Great Northern Railway to the northbound trails, early visitors came to capture the essence of wilderness and to experience personal challenges. Some took 14-day expeditions through the park, taking the time to "live" a bit of Glacier. Pack trips journeyed from East Glacier to the Lewis Hotel on Lake McDonald, by way of the network of chalets and tent camps. All of the lodges were a highlight — a touch of glamour in the wilderness. The Great Northern Railway ran a high-class operation where the venturesome were catered to and treated like royalty during their sojourn in the wilderness.

The Great Northern established this network of chalets and lodges and promoted them with advertising. "See America First" and "The Empire Builder" were successful marketing slogans. The railroad pinpointed the destination, facilitated the transportation, and provided the advertising in a concerted effort intended to create a surging interest and endless demand for the western bound "All Aboard!" for Glacier.

In 1911, one year after Glacier was established as a national park, 4,000 tourists visited. The first year Glacier Park Lodge was running, 12,138 tourists came to the park. Now, in the 1990s, Glacier National Park has the most visitors in its history, with the number of tourists exceeding two million each season.

The Great Northern's grand hotels and chalets still touch the hearts of millions of visitors who marvel each year at "Glacier's Grandest" — the log and stone structures that have graced Waterton-Glacier International Peace Park for over three quarters of a century.

Glacier
Park
Hotel

Lake
McDonald
Lodge

Many Glacier Hotel

Prince of
Wales
Hotel

At Glacier Park Station my wardrobe, which I had not seen for weeks, was put on the train. 'They do very well,' as the English say, in the West. Everything was pressed. Even my shoes had been freshly polished.

A crowd of people had gathered at the station...There were many good-byes. Then the train moved slowly off. I stood on the platform as long as I could and watched the receding lights. Behind the hotel rose the purple-black silhouette of the mountains, touched with faint gold by the lingering finger of the sun.

Mary Roberts Rinehart
Through Glacier Park, 1916

HISTORIC MAP, CIRCA 1920s.

About the Author

Bridget E. Moylan is a native Montanan whose seasons as an employee at Many Glacier Hotel and her love for Glacier National Park and its historic hotels and chalets inspired her to compile this history.

The author grew up in Missoula, Montana attending Loyola Sacred Heart High School and the University of Montana. She graduated from Carroll College, Helena, Montana, where she edited the campus paper, *The Prospector* and earned a Bachelor's degree in English writing, minoring in History. Her work has appeared in *Montana Outdoors*, *Colours* and other publications. Additional Montana publishing experience includes stints with the Montana Department of Fish, Wildlife and Parks of Helena, *Northern Lights* Magazine and Mountain Press Publishing of Missoula and the *Hungry Horse News* of Columbia Falls.

She is currently an Independent Sales Director with Mary Kay Cosmetics and works free lance in writing and desktop publishing.

LEFT TO RIGHT: JOHN AND VIOLET MOYLAN AND LIL DEVINE. THE MOYLANS, PATERNAL GRAND-PARENTS OF THE AUTHOR, MOTORED FROM OMAHA, NEBRASKA, WITH THE DEVINES IN 1940. AFTER SPLURGING ON BREAKFAST AT MANY GLACIER HOTEL, AT THE DARING PRICE (FOR THE DEPRESSION ERA) OF $1.00 EACH, THE FOUR-SOME TRAVELED TO WATERTON FOR THE DAY.

Vincent Devine Photo

BIBLIOGRAPHY

While no comprehensive history of all of the Great Northern Railway's hotels and chalets of Waterton-Glacier International Peace Park has been written, the buildings have been the focus of many local newspaper articles, books, stories, features and oral histories. The archives of Glacier National Park contributed substantial information. The author consulted the following sources for the information on *Glacier's Grandest*.

Historical Interviews
Beebe, Eva, 1975
Black, Margaret, 1984
Edkins, Helene Dawson, 1982
Gudger, Genevieve, 1975
Henderson, Mrs. Gonhild "Bud", 1977
Huffine, Dan, 1982
Hummel, Don, 1979
Hutchings, Cora P., 1962
Jennings, Charlie, 1977
Macomber, Bea, 1976
Neitzling, Ed, 1976
Opalka, Joe and Martha, 1975
Powell, Ace, 1976
Price, Dorothy Ray, 1975
Ruhle, Dr. George C., 1975, 1983
Staples, Mr. and Mrs. Merlin, 1979
Vincent, Ruth, 1975
Personal Interviews
Hegg, Larry, 1999
Hodgson, Jamie, 1999
Kendall, Joe, 1999
Luding, Kay, 1993
Millhouse, Gladys, 1993
Peek, Trudi, 1993

Buchholtz, C.W. *Man in Glacier*. Glacier Natural History Association, Inc., in cooperation with the National Park Service, West Glacier, MT, 1976.
Californian Pythian Star. November 1924. Flathead County Library, Kalispell Branch, Montana File.
Djuff, Ray. *The Prince of Wales Hotel.* Waterton Natural History Association, Alberta, Canada, 1991.
Dowler, J.W. *Lake McDonald*. Columbia Falls, MT, 1914.
_____, *Personal Journal*. Columbia Falls, MT, 1935.
Elwood, Henry. *The Train Didn't Stay Long.* Thomas Printing Inc., Kalispell, MT, 1982.
Glorious Glaciers, The Exciting Early History of Glacier National Park. Montana Heritage Series #9, Montana Historical Society Press, 1957-58.
Hagen, John, and Bundick, Tessie. *A History of Many Glacier Hotel*. Glacier Park Foundation, Minneapolis, MN, 1985.
Hanna, Warren L. *Montana's Many-Splendored Glacierland*. University of North Dakota Foundation, Grand Forks, ND, 1987. (First published by Superior Publishing Company, Seattle, WA, 1976.)

_____. *Stars over Montana: Men Who Made Glacier National Park History.* Glacier Natural History Association, West Glacier with Falcon Press Publishing Company, Helena, MT, 1988.

Holterman, Jack. *Historical Monographs: Mary, Mary Quite Contrary.* Glacier Natural History Association, West Glacier, MT, 1991.

Houk, Rose. *Going-To-The-Sun: The Story of the Highway Across Glacier National Park.* Woodlands Press, Division of Robert White & Associates, Delmar, with Glacier Natural History Association, West Glacier, MT, 1984.

Hummel, Don and Eugenia. *One Man's Life from Wagon Wheels to the Space Age.* Free Enterprise Press, Bellevue, WA, 1988.

Laut, Agnes C. *Enchanted Trails of Glacier Park.* Robert M. McBride & Company, New York, 1926.

McDonald Architects, James R. *Granite Park Chalet, Historic Preservation Architectural Guide.* Missoula, MT, 1985.

_____, *Lake McDonald Lodge, Historic Preservation Architectural Guide.* Missoula, MT, 1985.

_____, *Many Glacier Hotel, Historic Preservation Architectural Guide.* Missoula, MT, 1984.

_____, *Sperry Chalet, Historic Preservation Architectural Guide.* Missoula, MT, 1986.

_____, *Two Medicine Chalet, Historic Preservation Architectural Guide.* Missoula, MT, 1985.

McMillion, Bill. *Old Lodges and Hotels and Our National Parks.* Icarus Press, South Bend, IN, 1983.

Moynahan, J.M. *The Ace Powell Book.* J.M. Moynahan and Ace Powell Art Galleries Inc., Kalispell, MT, 1974.

National Parks Magazine. No. 86, Washington, D.C., July-Sept, 1946.

Ober, Michael J. *Enmity and Alliance: Park Service-Concessioner Relations in Glacier National Park, 1892-1961.* Master of Arts Thesis, University of Montana, 1973.

Rinehart, Mary Roberts. *Tenting Tonight in Glacier National Park.* The Riverside Press, Cambridge, MA, 1918.

_____, *Through Glacier Park: Seeing America First with Howard Eaton.* The Riverside Press, Cambridge, MA, 1916.

Robinson, Donald H. *Through the Years in Glacier National Park.* Glacier Natural History Association Inc., West Glacier, MT, 1960.

Shaw, Douglas V. "The Great Northern Railroad and the Promotion of Tourism," *Journal of Economics.* Vol. 13, No. 1, June, 1989.

Wood, Charles and Dorothy. *The Great Northern Railway.* Pacific Fast Mail, Edmonds, Washington, 1979.

Many thanks go to the numerous people who volunteered their time and knowledge to this project: Beth Dunagan and Deirdre Shaw at the Glacier National Park Library and Archives, Alex Lobdell, Colin C. Irvine, Bill Schuster, Richard and Beverly Dowler, Montana Historical Society, University of Montana Archives, and all those interviewed. For my parents, Tom and Mary Fran, my family, and friends. You know how you have encouraged me. Special thanks to Geoff for his endless strength and inspiration. And to all of those who have inquired about *Glacier's Grandest* in one way or another—you have all helped tremendously.

Bridget E. Moylan